SAINTS
FOR ALL
SEASONS

SAINTS
FOR ALL
SEASONS

VICTOR J. GREEN

AVENEL BOOKS
New York

This 1983 edition is published by Avenel Books,
distributed by Crown Publishers, Inc., by arrangement with
Blandford Press.

Manufactured in the United States of America

Library of Congress Cataloging in Publication Data

Green, Victor J.
  Saints for all seasons.

  Bibliography: p.
  Includes indexes.
  1. Christian saints—Biography.   I. Title.
BX4655.2.G73 1983   270′.092′2   [B]   83-3694

ISBN: 0-517-413027

h g f e d c b a

Contents

5

N.B. In the Alternative Services Book some dates are different, as follows:
[1]January 28, [2]July 11, [3]May 25, [4]July 6.

Foreword

There are so many books with stories of the saints that yet another may be considered superfluous. However, this book is designed for use as a handbook for readers who are looking for a concise story that makes some effort to distinguish between what is known to be true and what is probably legend. There is no need to apologise for legends, indeed they often have great teaching value. As I point out elsewhere in the book, Aesop's Fables are not true but we often turn to them to make a point about human behaviour and relationships. We may smile at the oddity of some of the legends but it is with a friendly, not a cynical smile. Sir Arthur Quiller-Couch once wrote, 'a legend however exaggerated beyond fact, is its own fact, witnessing belief'.

Inevitably in a book of this size, somebody's favourite saint is going to be left out and for that I apologise. From the thousands of saints I have chosen fifty-four, including the Gospel writers, the patron saints of Great Britain, many of the 'popular' saints and a fair proportion of those exciting saints of Britain who lived during the wild and dangerous days before the Norman Conquest.

The creation of a saint is by the process of canonization. In those early days local recognition became enlarged to recognition by the church. This is canonization achieved informally, or by long usage. From the tenth century, canonization came into the hands of the Bishop of Rome, the Pope. Nowadays there is a recognised process which the Catholic Church pursues. It is important to remember that a saint is not made by canonization but by the life and example of the saint. Saints are not perfect people, most indeed confess that they are far from it. Saints are measured by their personal lives which are considered to have been lived heroically in some way or another. It is acknowledged that there have been numerous lives which were saintly but have not been recognised by canonization.

7

Acknowledgments

My personal thanks are due to the staff of the Bodleian Library, Oxford, for their interest and assistance in directing me towards relevant source books, to Mr Terence Goldsmith of Blandford Press for his advice and encouragement, to Mrs Joan Ticer for her help with the design of the cover of this book and, once more, my unbounded thanks to my wife for her patience, skill and the time devoted to typing and re-typing my work so that it should be presented in immaculate style to the publisher.

Victor J. Green

SAINTS
FOR ALL
SEASONS

You have probably heard a person say that they are giving up something during the season of Lent. It may be something that seems fairly trivial, like not eating sweets, or not having sugar in their tea. It may be giving up free time to go to church services more often. Their purpose is to keep reminding themselves of the things Jesus gave up, including His own life for us. The season of Lent is chosen because it is connected with the forty days during which Jesus lived in the wilderness, free from all distractions, while he prepared Himself for His work in ministering to His people and founding the Christian faith.

There have always been religious people who go much further in self-sacrifice and self-denial, even to the point of death. These people are called 'ascetics'. One of the most famous of the ascetics is Simeon, a shepherd's son, living in Cilicia on the borders of Syria about 400 years after Jesus. He was a religious boy, thinking deeply about the life of Jesus while he looked after his father's sheep. From listening to Christian teachers he learnt about the words of Jesus, spoken during His Sermon on the Mount. These words were the Beatitudes: 'Blessed are the pure in heart', 'Blessed are the peace makers'. 'Blessed are those who mourn' . . . 'All these people,' said Jesus, 'will find happiness'. Simeon asked one of the preachers how he could find such happiness. He was told to pray, to fast, to suffer, and to lead a solitary life.

Simeon thought about this and, later, he had a dream. He dreamed that he was digging a foundation for a home. When he tried to stop, even to take a breath, he was urged to renew his efforts. At last, he had dug a foundation that would be deep enough for any structure, however tall. Indeed in his mind he saw a tall, slender, pillar.

After this experience, he asked to be admitted to a Chrisian monastery near at hand, ruled by an abbot called Timothy. At first his request was refused but he would not move from the gate, begging to be allowed to serve even as the lowliest servant in the monastery. Even the monks were amazed at his spiritual enthusiasm. He learnt all the psalms by heart, he went without food and water for long periods and, on one occasion, tied a tough rope, made of twisted fibres, around his waist until it cut into his body. Such was his suffering that the abbot turned him out of the monastery lest others should follow his example. He became more and more certain that to live a holy life he must get away from people. He made an enclosure for himself at the top of a hill. He lived there with little food and no shelter from the sun or rain. Visitors came from far and near to see and speak to this holy man. They wanted to touch him and ask for his prayers. This prevented him from being alone, so he built himself a pillar about 9 ft (2.7 m) high with a small platform to live on. Only the bare necessities of food and drink were sent up to him to keep him alive. He spent his time in prayer and meditation, but he still attracted visitors and followers who were amazed at his ability to live a holy life in such a way. The visitors tended to distract him and, in order to be further away from them, after four years he replaced his pillar with one that was 18 ft (5.5 m) high. The platform he lived on was little more than 6 ft (1.8 m) across, making it difficult for him even to lie full length when he slept. It was certainly fortunate that he did not walk in his sleep, although he had a railing all round the edge of his platform.

After three more years, he was still worried by the crowds of people who came, so he built a new pillar 30 ft (9 m) high and, after another ten years, he went up to 60 ft (18 m), with food and water being sent up by means of a pulley and chain. He managed to live like this for another twenty years.

Visitors came from far and wide, not so much out of curiosity but to admire his patience, his humility, his wisdom, and his saintliness, rather than his endurance. The Empress Theodosius came to seek his advice about her own religious life, and the Emperor Mercian visited in disguise. He died at the top of his pillar when he was sixty-nine years old. We should not, however, measure the goodness of Simeon by the way in which he endured suffering, which he accepted voluntarily, but by the perfection of his love, patience and humility. He urged those who came to see him to serve God in their own way in their daily lives and he had a great influence on non-believing barbarians who turned to the Christian way of life.

Many other holy men imitated Simeon and these came to be known as the 'pillar saints'.

The Greek word for pillar is *Stylos*, this is why he is called Simeon the Stylite.

St Benedict (Benet)   (b. *c.*628)   *12 January*

This saint is known by a number of names. It would be as well to say from the start that he is not the Benedict who founded the Benedictine Order, associated with Monte Cassino.

He was first named Biscop Baducing and, as a young man of noble birth, served at the court of King Oswy of Northumbria. When he was twenty-five years old he made a journey to Rome with Wilfrid. After a second visit (he went five times altogether) he went on to Lerins to live the life of a monk, taking the name of Benedict. This monastery was renowned for its strict rules of life and regular discipline. He spent three years there before he was ordered by Pope Vitalian to return to England with Theodore, the new Archbishop of Canterbury, and Adrian. During this period, including visits to Rome, Benedict built a library and a collection of sacred relics and pictures. After being Abbot of St Peter and St Paul's in Canterbury, he went back to his native Northumbria. He was inspired to build his own monastery and, on land given to him by King Egfrid, he founded one at Wearmouth, dedicated to St Peter. Some years later, a sister house at Jarrow was dedicated to St Paul.

These monasteries were built of stone, with the aid of French craftsmen brought over specially. Buildings in northern England at this time were usually wooden. Even the church at Lindisfarne was of wood, covered with a thatch of straw and reeds. Another inovation by Benedict was to employ glaziers to put glass in the windows, something that was entirely new in the buildings of those days. Saxon architecture owes much to his initiative and invention.

From his library, and other collections, the monasteries had books and pictures. At Wearmouth there were notable pictures of Mary, the Apostles, the gospel stories and the Revelation.

At Jarrow there was a series of pictures illustrating the harmony and connection between the Old and the New Testaments. For instance, one pair of pictures drew a parallel between Isaac carrying wood for his own sacrifice and Jesus carrying the wooden cross for his crucifixion.

After one of his visits to Rome, he returned with the Precentor of St Peter's to teach his monks the arts of Gregorian chanting and Roman ceremonial singing. His two monasteries became the best furnished and equipped in Europe. One of Benedict's pupils was Bede, whose later work was made possible by Benedict's extensive library.

He also organised the writing of the manuscript of the Bible, a manuscript that was later taken as a present to Pope Gregory II. Benedict Biscop, or simply Benet as he was sometimes called, played a very important part in the development of the church in northern England.

In about 686 Benedict was stricken with paralysis of the lower limbs and this condition gradually worsened. For three years he lay crippled and suffering, confined to his bed and eventually almost entirely lost the use of his voice. Even so, to the stream of monks and others who came to see him, he indicated that he was joining their prayers and praise with his heart, if not with his voice. Although so ill, he was patient and true to his faith to the end. He was modest about his achievement for he once wrote, 'You must not think that the rules you have received from me were of my own devising, for I have visited seventeen well-ordered monasteries and chosen the best of their rules to leave you as my legacy'.

He died on 12 January in 690. William of Malmesbury records that the relics of Benedict rest at Thorney Abbey, although the monks of Glastonbury claim that part of them, at least, rest there.

St Kentigern (Mungo)   (b. *c*.518)   *14 January*

According to legend, Kentigern very nearly did not live at all, for when his mother, Thaney, a Scots lady of royal birth, was discovered to be expecting a baby, whose father was not known, the people were so shocked and angry that they were prepared to hurl her down from the top of a very steep hill, possibly the place now known as Traprain Law, near Haddington. She would certainly have died and the child would never have been born. Fortunately, she was helped to escape and the best that her friends could do was to put her into a coracle and push her out into the Firth of Forth. The tide took her across to the opposite shore of the estuary, to Culross, where a man called Serf, who himself eventually became recognised as a saint, looked after her until the baby was born.

Serf was very fond of the baby and caled him Mungo, which means 'little dear'. His mother gave him the name Kentigern. He was brought up by his mother in solitude. Since he enjoyed being alone, when he grew older he retired to a lonely spot called Glasghu, now known as Glasgow and not so quiet!

His mother brought him up in the Christian faith which he followed ardently and, like it or not, a community grew up around him. In time, when the need arose for a leader of this Christian community, the people wanted Kentigern to be their bishop and, unwillingly, he was so appointed.

As bishop he had to travel frequently to reach all parts of his diocese but he never neglected his prayers and readings. He would sometimes practise extreme austerity, standing in a stream of ice-cold water while he went through some of the daily services.

He was not always popular with the local tribal chieftains since they felt that he undermined the loyalty of their people. Eventually Kentigern was driven into exile.

Legend has it that he fled to Wales and may have accompanied David for a while. It is also said that he founded a monastery at Llanelwy and that Asaph put himself under Kentigern's direction. Welsh people tend to deny that Kentigern was there at all and certainly we have no proof. The name Kentigern does not appear in this district so it must be considered very doubtful whether he ever visited Wales.

However, he appears again at Glasgow, possibly after a short spell at Hoddern in Dumfrieshire. There is evidence that during this period there was a meeting between Kentigern and Columba; the story goes that they met and exchanged croziers, the staffs carried by bishops.

There is a charming tale of a miracle performed by Kentigern at this time, a reminder of which is perpetuated in the presence of a ring and a fish in the coat of arms of the city of Glasgow.

King Rydderch had given his queen a ring but one day he saw the ring on the finger of one of his knights who was sleeping. Angry and jealous, the king took the ring from the finger of the knight and flung it into the sea. King Rydderch then asked his queen to produce the ring which he had given her as a present. Of course, the queen was very upset knowing that she could not produce the ring, so she asked Kentigern what she should do. Kentigern told one of his monks to take out a boat and bring back to him the first fish that he caught. The fish, a salmon, was duly brought and, when it was cut open, there, inside, was the ring which the fish had swallowed. Thus the queen was able to take the ring and display it to her king. He must have been greatly surprised. (I am not sure that miracles performed to deceive are necessarily good ones.) However, the coat of arms of the city of Glasgow owes its origin to this legend. Kentigern also performed many other miracles which were more obviously commendable.

Kentigern died in about 603. There is a curious story that he died while taking a hot bath, on a day when he was due to baptise a multitude of people. His feast day is observed in Scotland as the first Bishop of Glasgow and he is also celebrated in Liverpool, Salford, and Lancaster.

St Sebastian (3rd Century) *20 January*

Sebastian is one of the early Christian martyrs about whom we know very few facts with certainty. He is relatively well known because so many artists have made his legendary exploits the subject of their paintings. He was a popular subject particularly among the Renaissance artists.

The only part of his story that is certainly true is that he was killed for being a Christian during one of the Roman persecutions and that he was buried beneath the Appian Way, which is one of the roads leading into Rome. However, the legend of his life is well worth telling and it is interesting to ponder how so much imaginary detail can develop.

He was born at Narbonne, in the Roman province of Gaul, and from his youth he was a keen servant of Jesus Christ. He joined the Roman army not because he wanted to fight for his emperor but because he felt that there he could best recruit soldiers for Christ. Some versions of the story of Sebastian declare that this was in A.D. 283 in the time of Emperor Carinus who was not so severe with Christians as Diocletian who followed him. Indeed, when Marcus and Marcellian were under sentence of death, Sebastian pleaded for them, unfortunately without success. Even so, Sebastian was not punished for his action. Some Christians, who knew that Sebastian was a follower of Christ, brought to him a woman called Zoe who had lost the power of speech. Sebastian prayed for her and she recovered. As a result of this, the husband of Zoe and the parents of Marcus and Marcellian, with sixteen other prisoners, were all converted to the Christian faith. One of the governors of the city of Rome became interested in Sebastian's beliefs and, after speaking with Sebastian, he too was received into the Christian faith. Consequently many Christian prisoners were released.

Emperor Carinus was succeeded by Diocletian, who inaugurated violent persecution of Christians. Hundreds were tortured and killed by the emperor's guards. Strangely enough, Diocletian was not aware that Sebastian was a Christian and promoted him to be Captain of the Pretorian Guard, a great honour since this was one of the crack Roman regiments.

The persecution of the Christians under Diocletian became fiercer and Zoe was arrested. She was put to death in a most horrible way — she was stifled by being hung by her heels over a fire. Other Christians were being stoned, beheaded, thrown into the sea, buried alive or stretched on the rack. Even the Pope and his officials were compelled to conceal themselves for fear of their lives during this massive persecution.

Sebastian gained admission to the presence of the emperor and declared his faith, protesting at the treatment of Christians. Diocletian was furious to find that the man he had honoured was a Christian and ordered his arrest. Sebastian was taken out to face the archers of Mauretanus. His body was riddled with arrows and left at the roadside. The widow of another martyr, Irene, preparing to have her husband's body buried found Sebastian and, to her delight, he was still alive. She took him to her house where he slowly recovered. As soon as he was well enough, he took up a position on a stairway where he knew the emperor was bound to pass. As Diocletian arrived, Sebastian, in a loud voice, denounced him for his persecution of the Christians. For a moment the emperor was speechless for he had imagined that Sebastian was dead. Sebastian was arrested once more and, on the orders of the emperor, he was beaten to death with clubs.

Another of Sebastian's followers, a lady called Lucina, had his body buried in the catacombs below the Appian Way. Today, a beautiful church, dedicated to St Sebastian, stands above the spot where his body lies.

His emblem is an arrow and it is no surprise to find that Sebastian is the patron saint of archers and soldiers.

St John Chrysostom (b. *c.*347)   *27 January*

Sometimes those in authority, even within the church itself, are disturbed when their authority, and the way it is used, is challenged. However truthful and correct the criticism is, the ruling powers do their best to silence it. John Chrysostom was one who suffered in this way. He really was too good for those he dared to criticise and, sad as it is to report, his own fellow Christians were responsible for his death.

John was a brilliant teacher and speaker. The surname Chrysostom was bestowed on him later. (*Chrysostom* means golden Mouth.) He was born in about A.D. 347 in Antioch, in Syria. His father was a high-ranking army officer who died soon after John's birth. He was brought up by his mother, a devout Christian, but it was his first intention to be a lawyer. John was such a proficient speaker that during his training he was said to be better than his masters.

When he was eighteen, he suddenly changed his mind and told his mother that he was going to take the first steps towards living a monastic life. He was baptised and received minor orders, halfway to becoming a priest. His mother persuaded him to stay at home for a while but, after her death, he lived as a hermit monk in a cave. He spent two years alone, praying, meditating, fasting and wandering. He was compelled to return to the city when he was dangerously ill and it was then that he was persuaded to be ordained. He served as deacon and then, at the age of forty-two, he bacame a priest. He was most noted for his ability as a preacher, talking about the gospels in such a way that everyone could understand. He used easy, topical and familiar examples; we find that much of what he said to his listeners over 1,600 years ago is as relevant today as it was then. He preached several times a week and sometimes even several times a day. There were in Antioch at that time about 100,000 Christians, comprising half the population of the city.

John has been honoured as one of the four great Greek doctors of the church. He was critical and outspoken about the misuse of the wealth of the church and criticised many of the wicked practices at the emperor's court and he did not spare Theophilus, the Archbishop of Alexandria, whose style of life was luxurious and extravagant.

Theophilus hoped to become even richer by being the next Bishop of Constantinople, a city noted for its wealth, vice, lavish spectacle and entertainment. However, in 398, John was appointed to that high office and immediately put into practice all the ideals he had preached. He wore the ordinary dress of a monk, and his gown was probably the shabbiest to be seen. The way of life in the bishop's household became very severe and economical with much less money spent on food and entertainment, leaving more for distribution among the poor. He preached unceasingly against extravagant living, not sparing the noble, the rich, or his fellow priests. It was because of his brilliant speaking at this period that he gained the nickname 'Chrysostom'. He visited hospitals, prisons, and took up lawsuits in which poorer people might not have been able to defend themselves. He was not popular among the rich, or among his fellow bishops and other clergy, who saw in his way of life a criticism of theirs.

The empress and Theophilus plotted to overthrow John. Theophilus saw his chance when he expelled some Egyptian and Syrian bishops who then came to John Chrysostom for help. John sympathised with them and Theophilus was called to give account of himself. However, when the case was heard, through the double dealing of Theophilus, John found that he was the one to be confronted with a list of charges, hastily made up. The emperor sent John into exile, but such was John's popularity that the people rioted and, by coincidence, an earthquake occurred at this time. These events influenced the emperor to annul his verdict and John stayed on.

However, John's enemies were soon hard at work again, aiming to put him in the emperor's disfavour. John had protested at the extravagance of casting a silver statue of the empress and it was not difficult for his enemies to force his deposition. An order was made banishing him to Armenia, a desert area between the Caspian and the Black Sea.

Even in exile, John maintained contact with his friends and wrote about 200 letters, which remain as evidence of his outstanding spirituality. He sometimes dared to visit his friends, so that his enemies had to persuade the emperor to order him to even more distant banishment in the Caucasus.

Then, ill and exhausted, John set out on the road to Iberia. The journey was too much for him and he died on the road from exhaustion in 407. He was buried in a little chapel dedicated to a martyr. The emperor and empress must have been shocked by this and sought to make amends by bringing his remains back to Constantinople, where they were buried with all due solemnity.

John was not a martyr who died because he would not give up his faith. He was a martyr because of his own goodness and sincerity.

St Scholastica (b. *c.*480) *10 February*

Scholastica was the sister, possibly the twin sister, of Benedict whose feast day is 21 March and whose story is told elsewhere in this book. It has to be admitted that, apart from this, we know little about Scholastica. However, Gregory allotted two chapters of his book *Dialogues* to her and we must suppose that what he wrote about her is partly true and partly the traditional stories that grew up around her. In any case, this is the only source that we have.

We can be sure that from an early age she devoted her life to the service of God, living some of her early years within a community. After her brother had moved to Monte Cassino she moved into the same district and founded a nunnery, eventually being installed as abbess. She used to leave her community once a year in order to visit her brother, but as she could not enter his monastery, their meeting place was a little house outside Benedict's monastery. Here they would enjoy each other's company, talk as brother and sister, and spend time together in prayer and praise of God. No doubt they also talked abut the day-to-day difficulties of running a community.

On the last occasion on which they met, they passed the day as usual and then sat down to supper before taking their leave of each other and returning to their own community. Scholastica sensed that this was to be their last meeting and she suggested that her brother should extend the visit by staying at the house until the next day. Benedict, however, felt that this would be breaking one of the rules he had laid down for his own monks, and so refused.

Scholastica, disappointed, bowed her head on her hands and

quickly asked God to persuade her brother to stay. Hardly had she finished her prayer, when a great thunderstorm arose, with howling winds and rain. Benedict realised that he could not make the journey back to Monte Cassino that night. 'God forgive you, sister,' he exclaimed, 'whatever have you done?' Scholastica relied. 'I asked a favour of you, and you refused. So I asked God for a favour and he granted it.'

Benedict had to stay and they spent most of the night talking about the joys they experienced through giving their lives to the service of God and the church. They parted the next morning and Benedict did not see his sister alive again. Three days later, Benedict was alone at prayer when he had a vision of a dove flying up into the sky. He knew at once that the dove was the spirit of his sister. Benedict was not unhappy about this. Of course, he was sad that he would not be able to see her and talk to her again but he was certain that after death they would meet in another, spiritual, way.

He gave thanks to God for her life and then told the brothers in the monastery. He had prepared a tomb for himself in the monastery at Monte Cassino but he sent some of his monks to fetch her body and place it in the grave meant for him. In this way, he was saying that just as they had been so close to each other in life, so they would be in death. Her relics have since then been removed, and, together with those of her brother, now rest in France, at Le Mans.

Although we know so little about Scholastica, she is worthy of a place in a calendar of saints simply as the sister of Benedict.

St Ethelbert (b. *c.*560)   *25 February*

At the time of Ethelbert, who was King of Kent in the sixth century, it was common for the ruler to enforce his wishes on his people, particularly in the matter of faith. The king was accustomed to dictating the religious beliefs and practices of the ordinary folk but Ethelbert was an exception and did not do this.

While on a visit to the Continent, Ethelbert, who was at that time a pagan, met Bertha, the daughter of Charibert, king of Paris. She was, however, a Christian, and when she came to Kent as the wife of King Ethelbert, he allowed her to bring a French priest, Liudhard, with her. He became a bishop and officiated in her church in Canterbury, dedicated to St Martin.

Bertha was a good, pious lady and influenced the king without actually persuading him to become a Christian. He was becoming interested in her religion however, when word came that Pope Gregory, was sending Augustine to England to preach the Christian faith and to convert the people of this country to Christianity.

Ethelbert allowed Augustine and his followers to land on the Isle of Thanet, indicating that he would meet his visitors there to discuss their purpose in coming to England. He insisted that the conference should take place out of doors, where he felt they would be less likely to practise magic on him than if they met in a church. He was still very pagan in his outlook. Ethelbert sat under an oak tree and listened carefully to all they had to say. After the conference he told Augustine that he and his priests could freely go about his kingdom and teach, preach and convert. Ethelbert did not try to influence his people, insisting that to serve Jesus Christ must be a free decision. He himself had been very impressed by Augustine and was gradually won over to the Christian way of life. The king and many of his nobles were baptised on Whit Sunday in 597. Inevitably, as soon as it was known that the king was now a Christian, the people of Kent also were converted in hundreds.

Ethelbert was determined to put the welfare of his people first so his laws were fair and just, setting a pattern for succeeding ages. Lands and buildings at Canterbury were donated to Augustine and his growing church. The king put no pressure on his people to become Christian for he realised that the service of Jesus Christ must be voluntary and that belief is something that cannot be enforced. Not only did Ethelbert build the cathedral church of Christ in Canterbury itself, but outside the walls he built the abbey and church of St Peter and St Paul (afterwards called St Augustine).

At Rochester, Ethelbert built another cathedral in honour of St Andrew and influenced the neighbouring king of the East Saxons, Sabert, into becoming a Christian also. In London, the chief town of the East Saxons, Ethelbert built the first cathedral dedicated to St Paul.

Ethelbert was the most forward looking ruler in southern England at the time and his code of laws by which he ruled his people is one of the earliest known among such documents.

In 616 Ethelbert died and was buried at Canterbury, in the church of St Peter and St Paul which he had built and where already Queen Bertha and Bishop Liudhard were buried. Such was his fame and popularity that from then up to the time of Henry VIII a lamp was kept burning in his memory.

The most surprising thing about King Ethelbert was his modern approach to the practice of kingship. He never forced his people to follow his example. His believed that the world would only become Christian by proper teaching and example, never by force or compulsion.

St David (b. *c.*520) *1 March*

David is the Anglicised form of Dewi, which was his real name, and, for this short life, the more familiar form will be used. Unfortunately, there is no early account of the life of this patron saint of Wales, possibly the most celebrated of British saints. All that exists to provide early information are accounts based on a biography written about 1090 by Rhygyfarch, son of Bishop Sulien of St David's. Rhygyfarch was a learned man who claimed that he had earlier sources, but these are not specified and it must be admitted that it is difficult to distinguish the historical fact from the fable.

David, like many other saints of this period of British history, was the son of a *Sant*, a Welsh prince, born in the area now called Dyfed, possibly in Henfynw. This was a golden age in the history of Welsh Christianity when many sons of high birth found that their belief led them to a monastic life. Cadoc was one who founded Llencarfan, while Illtyd left his military career to lead the celibate life of a soldier for Christ. He was probably the model from whom the story of Galahad is taken. Certainly, Illtyd founded a monastery at Llantwit, and it was to this centre of Christian life that David came. There is a story that one of the old holy men, Paulinus, lost his sight following a severe illness. Some of his pupils and disciples looked into his eyes to try to find the reason for this affliction. David would not because he maintained that he had never raised his eyes to his master's face. Paulinus commended him for this but, nevertheless, asked David to touch his eyes and bless them. This action restored sight to Paulinus.

David's biographer then attributes a number of activities to his subject, many of which must be open to some doubt. If Rhygyfarch is to be believed, David founded twelve monasteries to the glory of God, from Glastonbury and Bath, to Croyland, Repton, Leominster, Raglan and Llangyfelach.

However, when David was thirty years old we can be sure that he founded his own monastery at Mynyw, or Minevia. After David's death this place came to be known as St David's. The Celtic hermits and monks loved to find remote, wild, almost inaccessible places for the great centres of Christianity, but from these centres there was constant travel to people, even at a great distance, to reform and convert those who had not heard the message of Christianity.

The monastic rule at Minevia was very strict. The monks had only one meal each day, bread, vegetables, eggs, milk and water. Most of the day was spent in strict silence. Unusually for those days, there was no alcoholic drink, and for this reason David's monks were known as 'The Watermen'. For the work in the fields, David allowed no oxen, declaring that every man was his own ox. They followed a strict rule of attendance at services and David himself would often pray through the night, placing before God the needs of all people.

Even so, David was not a killjoy. In fact, wherever he went he spread good humour and fun. He also must have had a wonderful voice. The Bishop of Llandaf called a great meeting of church leaders and people, called a Synod, probably to discuss a breakaway group from the true teaching of the church. The crowds were enormous and when the bishop tried to talk to them all, he could not be heard by those furthest from him. A number of other speakers tried, but without success. Then David was called to speak. He did not want to at first, but at last he consented. His brilliant voice, like a trumpet, could be heard by everyone. A later elaboration of this story says that a mound of earth sprang up from the ground so that all could see him as well. It is reported, and it is probably true, that a white dove perched itself on his shoulder while he talked.

The Bishop of Llandaf became Archbishop of Caerleon and, when he died, David succeeded him. He could not leave his monastery at Mynyw, so a new cathedral was built there. Today that site is known as St David's a great cathedral with its Norman nave, set among ruins dating back to the sixth century, with the remains of little chapels dotted around. When the news that David was dying went out, crowds came from all over Wales to be near. His last message was, 'Brothers and sisters, be joyful and keep your faith and do the little things that you have seen and heard with me'. He was buried in the cathedral-abbey church, probably on March 1, 589.

Miraculous events have been connected with David and, in particular, he is said to have produced a flow of fresh water from the ground on several occasions. The most important of these is at Ffynnon Feddyg where he also performed miracles of healing.

The national emblem of Wales is David's flower — the daffodil.

St Chad   (b. *c.*620)   *2 March*

Chad, or Ceadda as he is sometimes known, was one of four Christian brothers, two of whom became bishops. Cedd, his brother, was founder of Lastingham Abbey in Yorkshire and later Bishop of the East Saxons.

Chad was an Angle, born in Northumberland, and a Christian trained by Aidan at Lindisfarne. His early work was with the Irish but he was recalled to take charge of Lastingham

Abbey, a wild and solitary place on the Yorkshire moors, near Whitby. He succeeded his brother Cedd, who moved south and founded many monasteries, including Bradwell-on-Sea, and Tilbury in Essex.

King Oswy then called Chad to become Bishop of York. There was some confusion over this appointment since, at the same time, King Oswy's son had designated Wilfrid to that appointment. However, the king had his way and Chad devoted his life to truth, purity, humility and self-denial. He would not travel on horseback but, to reach all parts of his province and to be available to all, he walked, in the manner of the apostles. He preached wherever he found himself, in towns, villages, cottages and castles.

In 699, or thereabouts, Theodore was appointed to Canterbury and the former controversy arose, but this time Theodore supported Wilfrid, declared that Chad had been improperly consecrated, and turned him out of York. Chad accepted the decision humbly. He declared, 'If you consider that I have not been properly consecrated, I willingly resign this charge of which I never thought myself worthy. I undertook it, though unworthy, under obedience.' This acceptance so impressed Theodore that when it was necessary to appoint a new bishop at Lichfield, for the area of Mercia, it was Chad who was appointed. Chad had already built a house of retreat near the church in Lichfield and he often retired there to pray, read and converse with some of his fellow monks.

Chad did not live much longer but, in the short space of three years, he impressed all with his administration and his own holiness in life, to such an extent that he gained a great number of converts.

He would have continued to travel on foot but this was getting so difficult for him that Theodore insisted that he travel on horseback. Chad founded a house of retreat and a monastery, probably at Barrow-upon-Humber. He knew that he would not live much longer and, after he experienced a dream in which he said that he heard wondrous singing, he called his monks together. He urged them to keep the rules of their order and live peaceably together. He told them that the end of his life was near. A few days later he died.

His life made a great impact on Christians in England and this is evident from the fact that thirty-one churches and numerous wells in the Midlands are named after him.

There are many legends about Chad. In one of them it is said that he was praying near a stream when a deer that was being pursued by hunters dashed into the clearing where Chad was. He sent it off into the forest and then stood in the way of the hunters. He talked to them and persuaded them not to chase after the deer. They agreed and continued talking to Chad. In no time at all he had converted them and accepted them by baptism into the Christian Church. This episode is often reproduced in art.

Another story tells us that he was known to two sons of King Wulfhere, a king who had been Christian but had reverted to his pagan faith. Chad told the boys about the Christian faith and they were converted. When he heard this, King Wulfhere murdered the two boys in a fit of rage. Chad approached the king and, after making him see how wrong he was, brought him back into the church. Wulfhere, to show his repentance, founded an Abbey at Peterborough. The story does seem far-fetched, yet there is an entry in the Anglo-Saxon Chronicle that lists the name of Wulfhere as contributing to the endowment of Peterborough Cathedral.

Chad's relics lie in Birmingham Cathedral which bears his name, and Chad's Gospel, a seventh-century manuscript, is housed in Lichfield Cathedral Library.

St Thomas Aquinas (b. *c.*1225)   *7 March*

Thomas Aquinas was born into the noble family of the Counts of Aquino, which could trace its ancestry back through the centuries to the great Lombard families of Italy, His father was Sir Landulf and his mother was of noble Norman birth. He was born in the castle of Rocca Secca, whose ruins can still be seen in the hills rising above the little town of Aquino.

Thomas had three older brothers and some sisters. When

Thomas was quite young he was sleeping in a room next to his youngest sister, when she was killed by lightning. Although Thomas was unhurt, the memory of that incident stayed with him all his life and he always confessed to a fear of lightning and sudden death. During thunderstorms he would seek shelter and sanctuary in a church, not emerging until the storm had abated. This has given rise to a devotion to Thomas by those seeking protection from storms and from sudden death, just as many people seek the protection of Christopher against misfortune and accident when they travel, by carrying a St Christopher.

Because Thomas had made up his mind, when he was very young, to devote his life to the service and worship of God, he visited the Benedictine monastery at Monte Cassino which was only a few miles from his brithplace,. This was a holy place of great renown whose abbot at that time was Landulf Simbaldo, related to the Aquinas family. Thomas was admitted and lived there under the protection of Landulf from the age of six to thirteen.

He left there to study for five years at the University of Naples where he became interested in the work of another body of monks called the Order of Preachers. The Preachers were Dominican monks who travelled about the countryside to do their work, meeting people and working among them in their own families and communities. The Benedictines tended to live in a confined order, in the devotion to a life of work, prayer and worship within their own walls. The monks of the Order of Preachers were greatly impressed by Thomas and some declared that they saw 'a light around his head'. Father John of San Ghulians said of him, 'God has given you to our Order'.

Thomas's family were opposed to him joining any order other than Benedictine and did everything they could to make him change his mind. This interference went on for over two years. His mother followed him to Naples on one occasion, in an effort to persuade him to leave his order. Failing in this, she learnt that he was preparing to go on a journey to Rome and, with a small group of companions, travelling on foot. She sent his brothers to intercept and capture him, bringing him back a captive to Rocca Secca. Even so, locked away in a small room, Thomas used this period of captivity to write, read, and learn sections of the Bible by heart. On one occasion it seems that the brothers tried to distract him by sending a girl into his room. Thomas snatched a burning brand from the fire and chased her out. Eventually the family realised that they could not possibly influence Thomas, so he was released and allowed to return to the Order of Preachers.

Thomas then spent some years travelling in France and Germany, studying at schools and universities. In classes, he tended to listen rather than talk and because he was so silent and reserved, the other students and the tutors got the impression that he was dull and stupid. Thomas was a big man, with massive frame and fresh complexion. They called him 'a dumb Sicilian ox'. However, on one occasion, the papers on which he was writing his notes spilled over on to the floor and a fellow student helped to gather them together. He could not help reading some of them and was amazed at the learning and scholarship they showed. Then students began to open discussions with him and when he showed that he was able to unravel and make clear even the most obscure passages, they told their tutor about Thomas and what they had discovered. He gave Thomas a test whose results were astounding. 'We called Brother Thomas an ox', he said, 'but I tell you he will yet make his lowing heard to the uttermost parts of the earth'.

Thomas's reputation grew. He lived during a period of great argument within the Church about worship and belief. He did much to clarify theological ideas. Even popes asked for his opinion and at great general councils he was asked to expound on church issues. All the time he was writing. He gave to the church and to the world great works like, *Dissertations on the Lord's Prayer*, *Commentaries on the Scriptures*, and *Summae Theoligicae*. His works fill twenty thick volumes.

He was always patient and good-tempered, however much he was provoked or misunderstood. He had great humility, genuinely believing that others were more clever than he, and never attempted to belittle anyone.

In 1272 he fell ill while saying Mass on St Nicholas Day. He

knew that he was dying and declared, 'The end of my labour
has come.' Thomas was taken to the abbey at Terracina. Even
as he died he declared that all his life, his work, his studies,
had been for the glory of God.

He was made a saint by the Church in 1323. The Dominican
community did not gain possession of the saint's body until
1368 when he was buried with great ceremony at the cathedral
of Saint Serlin.

St Patrick (b.*c.*385)   *17 March*

Patrick was of Romano-British origin, his father, Calpurnius,
being a deacon and local municipal officer of some standing.
His grandfather had been a priest of the local community and
the family had been nominally Christian for some time. There
had been an earlier Patrick sent by Pope Celestine to work in
Ireland, who worked there for thirty years, and the two are
sometimes confused.

Patrick is reported to have been born in a place called
Bonnavem Taberniae and this has been variously identified as
Dumbarton, Cumberland or Glastonbury, but we cannot be
sure about any. We can be sure that the west of England was
often at the mercy of pagan marauders and pirates and that,
when he was sixteen, Patrick was captured during one of these
raids and sold as a slave to a chieftain in the west of Ireland.
Patrick confesses that until that time he had not known the
true God and had lived a thoughtless, irreligious life. He was
set to work as a herdsman and as his body endured hardship so
his spirit grew. He meditated on his Christian belief and in
particular considered the mystery of the Christian doctrine of
the Trinity, that God is one, yet God has three persons, or
aspects, the Father, the Son and the Holy Spirit. Six years
were spent as a herdsman in Mayo, at a place later called
Crochan Aigli (Croagh Patrick). He said, 'Constantly I used to
pray in the daytime. My faith grew and my spirit stirred. I said
as many as a hundred prayers a day and as many at night.'
Once in a dream he was told, 'Your ship is ready but not at

hand.' Eventually, he escaped and made his way across country covering nearly 200 miles to reach the sea. He found a ship but the sailors refused to take him and he turned unhappily away. He said a prayer inwardly and, before he had gone many yards further, the sailors called him back and let him travel with them. They had a storm-tossed voyage for four or five days, landing eventually in a wild place, where there was no food and the crew feared they would starve. They turned on Patrick and threatened him unless he could do something. 'You're a Christian, why don't you pray for some food now that we are starving to death.' Patrick calmly replied, 'Turn in good faith to God. Ask Him to send in food today.' Happily, immediately after that, a herd of wild pigs crossed their path and they were able to capture some of them for food. They also came across honey which was very welcome. Patrick was not quite so unpopular.

He returned to his family but he now knew that his destiny was to serve Ireland and spread the message of Christianity in that land. He first trained to become a priest, probably serving for some time at Lerins (near Cannes) and there is a possibility that some time during his training he visited Rome and saw the Pope. Pope Celestine had sent Palladius to Ireland but he had been killed and it seems that the next pope, Germanus, wanted Patrick to attempt the dangerous work.

Patrick travelled widely in Ireland but his efforts met with little success at first. The story goes that the turning point came when the pagans, led by the High King Laoghaire, celebrated an important heathen festival. At this festival all lights and fires had to be extinguished and no flame or light was to be seen until a burning brand was carried from the king's hall. It happened that this took place on the eve, or vigil, of the Christian Easter, and it was at this time that the Paschal (or Easter) candle was lit to represent the risen Christ. When all was dark and the light from the king's hall was awaited, Patrick lit the Paschal candle proclaiming the resurrection of Jesus Christ. The pagans were very angry and vowed to kill those who had lit the flame. Unafraid, Patrick and his fellow Christians met the king and his followers. Lengthy discussion took place and tolerance for the Christians was achieved. This was followed by conversion of the pagans and the estsablishment of a strong Christian church. Even so, Patrick had many enemies and as he travelled throughout Ireland his life was often in danger.

Some of his most dangerous encounters were with the Druids who saw their influence undermined by the Christians, but always it seemed that the force of Patrick's own character and the miracles attributed to him brought success. All over Ireland Christian churches were built, which were centres of Christian worship and civilization. In a biography of Patrick by Alban Butler, the writer declares, 'The name of Patrick is rightly rendered illustrious by the lights of sanctity with which the Church of Ireland shone during many ages and the colonies of saints with which it peopled foreign lands'.

Patrick died at Saul, on Strongford Lough, in about 461. In a period of less than thirty years he had brought about the conversion of Ireland to Christianity.

There is a story which may, or may not, be true that when he was finding difficulty in explaining that God is one, but also three in one — the mystery of the Holy Trinity — to illustrate the point, he picked up a shamrock and demonstrated that it had one leaf but that three parts made up the one leaf. This, it is said, is why the emblem of Ireland is the shamrock.

Patrick encouraged the founding of monasteries. He was vigorous in making them the centres of learning and culture for all the people. Patrick provides for us a model of determination and modesty, attributing all his success to God's grace.

He wrote a great deal and perhaps best known are the words, often used as a prayer, known as *Saint Patrick's breastplate:*

> I bind unto myself today
> The power of God to hold and lead
> His eye to watch, His might to stay
> His ear to hearken to my need
> The wisdom of my God to teach
> His hand to guide, His shield to ward,
> The Word of God to give me speech
> His heavenly host to be my guard.

St Joseph of Arimathea   (First Century)   *17 March*

Probably the only facts that are known about Joseph of
Arimathea are those recorded in the Bible. All four gospels
record that he was an influential, wealthy man who was
somewhat secretive about his regard for the teachings of Jesus.
He was a counsellor and a member of the Jewish Sanhedrin
which was instrumental in bringing about the Crucifixion,
although it appears that Joseph had not supported that
decision, since he himself was looking for a view of the
Kingdom of God which the ancient religion could not supply.
He was, then, a secret follower of Jesus, afraid of what might
happen to him if his belief became known. The death of Jesus
was a turning point, for this gave him courage and he boldly
went to Pontius Pilate asking to have the body of Jesus in order
to give it decent burial. His request was granted; the body of
Jesus was wrapped in fine linen and laid in a sepulchre, hewn
out of the rocky hillside, near Jerusalem. A stone was ready to
be rolled across to seal up the tomb. This tomb had been
prepared for Joseph himself and no body had lain in it before.
There is evidence that Joseph of Arimathea became a
companion of Philip, the apostle, and together they travelled
around, telling the story of Jesus, teaching His word and
converting people to Christianity.

One legend attaching to Joseph is that he was privileged to
be with Mary, the Mother of Jesus, when she died. There is a
belief that, because of her special life, the end of it was not by
death as we know it. The event is called the Assumption of
Our Lady.

From then on we only have legends about Joseph, written
long after his life, probably during the twelfth century,
although the writers may have had earlier sources.

Philip seems to have allotted Joseph the task of bringing the
Christian religion to Britain after Joseph had been imprisoned
on one occasion by a pagan king. Joseph, with another disciple
called Nicodemus, was put in a windowless cell from which
Joseph escaped, as if by a miracle. In the darkness of this cell,
Joseph must have been reminded of Jesus in the tomb and he
had a vision of the white grave cloths prepared for the body of

Jesus. At that, he experienced the feeling of being lifted by angels who deposited him outside the prison.

Joseph could now make his journey to Britain and he gathered about 600 disciples to accompany him. Joseph felt that they could work more effectively if they did not have the distractions of married life and so he asked them to promise to remain single. Only 150 of them promised to do so, and this smaller band set out for Britain. According to the story, the channel crossing was made easier for them since they all sailed on the shirt of one of Joseph's sons. This seems very strange and I wonder if somehow or other, as this story was told, the word 'ship' became confused with 'shirt'.

The Christian disciples first visited King Arviragus who ruled a great part of the south-west of Britain and, although he was not prepared to accept the truth of their teaching, he allowed Joseph and his followers to build a church at a place called Yniswitrin, the glassy isle, later called Glastonbury. There, Joseph and his followers were said to have been visited by the archangel Gabriel, who told them to build a church of wattle and daub in honour of Mary, the mother of Jesus. It would apear that this took place only thirty-one years after Jesus died and fifteen years after the Assumption of Mary.

At this point in the story, there seems to have been no mention of Joseph bringing with him the cup from which the disciples drank at the Last Supper with Jesus. The Grail has its origins in Celtic mythology, a cup which warriors passed round for them to drink together as a good luck charm, a talisman. The search for this has gone on ever since and some believe that it still exists somewhere in England.

The origins of the story that Joseph possessed this cup may be found in the record of John of Glastonbury, written in the fourteenth century, of the finding of a tomb at Glastonbury, which he reports as being of Joseph of Arimathea and his son, and in the detail he writes, 'In his tomb he had with him two cruets, white and silver, filled with the blood and sweat of the prophet Jesus'.

The truth is hidden from us by the passing of centuries, by decay, and by rebuilding, but certainly Britain must have had an acknowledged reputation in the fifteenth century for, at the great councils of the Christian Church at Constance and at Basle, the representatives from England were given precedence on the grounds that the people of that country must have accepted the teachings of Jesus Christ before any other people in Europe, teaching brought to them by Joseph of Arimathea.

True or not, all these accounts have some value for us. After all, Aesop's Fables are not true but they contain in them much which is wise and from which we can learn.

St Joseph   (First Century)   *19 March*

The story of Joseph is almost too well known to bear repetition. We know from the genealogy, or family tree, set out in the Gospels of St Matthew and St Luke that he was of royal descent. Indeed, he could trace his ancestry back to the great Jewish king, David. His son was truly born of David's line in Bethlehem, David's city, since the Romans had just decreed that all families should proceed to the town of their ancestors. On this journey, as on so many others, Joseph cared for Mary. Joseph was Mary's protector, for Joseph already knew that he was not the father of this baby who was to be born and that, indeed, there could be no earthly father for the Son of God. This was a mystery to Joseph but even when the neighbours gossiped and suggested that Joseph should desert Mary, he remained at her side as protector. Joseph then can be regarded as the privileged foster-father of Jesus who gave guidance and protection to the boy as he grew up.

Although the account of the visit of the wise men, the magi, to Bethlehem is included in the Christmas celebrations, in representations of the stable scene and on Christmas cards, it is likely that the visit did not take place until some time after the birth of Jesus. Herod, when he realised that a dangerous rival existed in Bethlehem, despatched his soldiers with orders to kill all male children under two yeras of age. If the massacre had immediately followed the birth of Jesus, there would not have been the need for such wholesale slaughter.

Even after this, the Holy Family stayed for a while in Egypt, so that Jesus must have been almost three years old when Joseph, Mary and their son finally returned to their home in Nazareth. There Jesus lived the life of an ordinary boy in a religious, Jewish home. He would have learnt much at his Mother's knee, played with the other children in the streets and countryside and eventually learnt his father's trade of carpenter.

The time came, as a boy of about eleven or twelve years, when he had to be presented at the Temple. This was a ceremony that is reflected in the Bar Mitzvah which Jewish boys still undertake. Bar Mitzvah means 'Son of the Law' and at this ceremony the boy is expected to discuss various aspects of his Jewish religion, demonstrating his knowledge of the Scriptures and of the Law. It was and still is an important stage in the Jewish youth's development. Joseph and Mary, with friends whose boys were about the same age, travelled to the Temple at Jerusalem, a journey taking several days. The boys were presented at the Temple where the High Priests questioned them and heard their answers. One can be sure that everyone took the opportunity to look around this wonderful city. After a day or two, the party would gather for the journey home. It is not surprising that as the group moved off, Mary and Joseph assumed that their son was among the group of boys collected together, laughing, playing and talking. The cavalcade had travelled a whole day before Jesus' parents realised that he was not with them. They hurried back, another day's journey, and looked for him in Jerusalem. They found him at last, absorbed in discussion with the learned men of the Temple. The priests were astounded at the learning displayed by the boy, something which says much for the teaching and influence of his parents. His Mother, Mary, was very worried indeed and almost scolded him. She said, 'Don't you understand that your father and I have sought you, sorrowing?' With these words she included Joseph in the boy's parentage. Jesus' answer is very significant. He said, 'Don't you know that I must be about my Father's business?' Jesus was not talking about being a carpenter, or village handyman. He was saying, for the first time, although only a boy of about twelve years of age, that he was declaring himself not only a son of the Law but also the Son of God.

Apart from these incidents, we don't know a great deal about Joseph that we can say is definitely true. We must be satisfied with the summing up in the New Testament that Joseph was a good man in every sense. We can also be fairly certain that Joseph died before the time came for Jesus to begin his three-year ministry that ended on the Cross. There is no mention of Joseph being with Jesus and Mary at the wedding in Cana. Certainly Joseph plays no part in the tragic end of Jesus' life.

The recognition of Joseph by the Church in its calendar comes very late; the first service in Rome celebrated in honour of Joseph appears in 1505, and it is likely that the prominence of Joseph in the mystery plays of the Middle Ages influenced this development.

The mystery plays, performed by craftsmen's guilds in this country, always gave Joseph a prominent place, probably because he was a craftsman himself.

In 1621 Pope Gregory XV made St Joseph's feast day a holiday of obligation.

St Cuthbert   (b. *c.*635)   *20 March*

Once more, we are indebted to Bede for what we know about the life of this saint, one of the many celebrated holy men who lived during the period before the Norman Conquest when the flames of Christianity spread rapidly through the British Isles. He was born in about 635 in the kingdom of Northumbria and was brought up by a widow in the village of Kenswith, with such love and care that Cuthbert always referred to her as his mother. His early years were spent in the neighbourhood of Melrose and he seems to have been exceptional both in intellect and physique. In all physical contests he was more than a match for his companions and because of this he tended to overlook his studies. Indeed, on one occasion when he was performing acrobatics with his fellows, a younger child was cross with him for not doing more school work. 'Oh Cuthbert,' he said, 'how can you waste your time in idle sport,

you, whom God has set apart to be a priest and a Bishop.'
This extraordinary prophecy stirred Cuthbert into taking his
studies more seriously. Fate seems to have decided things for
him also. He developed a condition in his knee which then
affected the nerves in his upper leg, finally crippling him so
that he could walk only with difficulty and pain. He recovered
from this condition but the experience made him determined
to give his life to God's service. Bede recounts that he
experienced remarkable answers to his prayers and that he had
miraculous visions. On one occasion, when a party of monks
were ferrying boatloads of timber to their monastery near the
mouth of the River Tyne, a storm arose that threatened to
wreck the boats. Cuthbert fell on his knees and prayed to God
for the safety of the boats and the monks. Almost at once the
wind dropped and the boats were saved.

A turning point in his life came when he was about thirty
years old. A glorious summer day was followed by an
unusually dark night. Cuthbert was alone at prayer when it
seemed to him that a beam of dazzling light shone across the
black sky. A company of angels and other spiritual beings
descended this beam, just as though it were a ladder. They
met another figure at the lowest part of the beam and then
returned, carrying this figure with them. The next day
Cuthbert learned that Bishop Aidan of Lindisfarne Abbey had
died during the night.

Cuthbert knew from then on what his vocation was to be. He
made his way to the monastery at Melrose and was accepted as
a monk by its prior, Boisil. He learnt much from the prior who
paid special attention to Cuthbert. Then one day the prior
urged Cuthbert to learn quickly for he, the prior, had only
seven days left to live. After seven days Boisil died,
prophesying that Cuthbert would become a bishop, strongly
echoing the prophecy of a young child years before.

Cuthbert became prior of the monastery. Apart from his
duties as prior, Cuthbert made innumerable missionary
journeys, on foot and on horseback, to preach to the people in
the north of England who were often hovering between their
former heathen customs and beliefs and this new faith called
Christianity. Cuthbert was a splendid preacher and his words

and actions brought many converts. There are stories of his ability to perform miraculous cures for the many sick who were brought to him. For all his fame, Cuthbert remained humble and often punished himself with over-long hours at work. He did not want the thanks, praise and compliments of the people to make him at all proud. To ensure this he would impose difficult tasks on himself. On one occasion, after he had been almost worshipped by a great crowd, he walked into the sea up to his armpits and spent the night praying to God. In the morning he came back on to the beach and knelt there. A monk who had watched Cuthbert through the night recounts that as the prior knelt on the beach two seals came up to him and played around his feet. Cuthbert blessed them and they went back to the sea.

Cuthbert seemed to have the same kind of affinity with the world of nature as Francis had. He scolded a flock of birds who kept eating the monastery's crop of barley. Obediently, they flew away and ate no more. Crows which had eaten out some of the thatch from his home were also scolded and, although they stayed to keep Cuthbert company, they never again destroyed the thatch.

Cuthbert was so well thought of that the Abbot transferred him to become Prior of Lindisfarne, a small island joined to the mainland by a causeway that was open only at low tide. He had a difficult time here, for the monks had not completely accepted the rule of the Christian Church from Rome and still kept ancient Celtic forms of worship. Cuthbert believed that the church should be world-wide and that local differences should be abandoned. Cuthbert did not force things but, eventually, his personality won the monks over.

He was there for twelve years before he moved to the island of Farne where he lived for another eight years as a hermit, a solitary monk. He built a rough dwelling which contained a small cell for him to live in and a little chapel, or oratory, for him to pray in. He received visitors and even provided a guest hut. Occasionally he made visits to the mainland.

Many people considered that this was a waste of his talents and eventually the King of Northumbria visited him and asked him to become the Bishop of Lindisfarne. Those former prophecies had come true. For two years Cuthbert served as a bishop, but he never gave up his simple life of prayer and service. Many instances were recorded of his power of prophecy and second sight, but his frugal life had taken its toll. He knew that death was near and asked to be allowed to return to his little hermitage on Farne. Many visited him, including the Abbot, but there was a period of stormy weather which lasted five days and when the Abbot was able to visit at last, he found Cuthbert very ill indeed in the guest house. The monks from Lindisfarne cared for him during his last days. 'When will you return?' they asked. 'When you take my body there,' he would reply. He died as he would have wished, at prayer in his remote little chapel. The monk who found him, according to an agreed plan, took two burning brands of wood and waved with them to signal across to Lindisfarne.

He was buried at Lindisfarne but years later, when the Danes invaded the north of England, his body was taken by the monks to Scotland. Many churches claim that the body of Cuthbert rested in them, if only for a night or two. That is why so many are named after him. Even a parish name like Kirkcudbright indicates that St Cuthbert rested there. Finally, the remains of Cuthbert were brought to Durham. Although the splendid shrine to St Cuthbert was plundered at the time of the Reformation, he is still at rest somewhere beneath the stones of Durham Cathedral.

St Benedict   (b. *c.*480)   *21 March*

For those who lived through the Second World War, and indeed for many since, the name Monte Cassino revives a vivid memory of the destruction of a beautiful monastery at the summit of a hill in Italy which stood in the way of the advancing allied troops. But, for centuries before that, and, happily, now again, it was the site of a centre of monastic life — a Benedictine monastery.

Benedict was born in about 480 into a middle-class family in central Italy. It was a turbulent time with the invading hordes of barbarian peoples breaking up the power of the Roman Empire, and growing divisions within the Christian church. Benedict was sent to Rome for his schooling but even at the age of fourteen he was devoutly Christian and realised that his life was to be devoted to prayer and praise of God. Among his fellow students he found vice and wickedness which revolted him.

He made his escape from Rome to join a small company of Christians who led a secluded community life and who soon recognised the unusual holiness of this young man. He did not enjoy their praise and adulation and removed himself even further from Rome to a cave on the mountain slopes of Subiaco where he enjoyed a life of solitude. He was attended by a monk called Romanus who brought him food and drink. He was sure that that was what God wanted him to do and, from then on, it seems he never refused to do anything, however hard or painful, that the voice of God in him demanded.

After about three years of solitude he began to attract attention and people came to him from quite distant places to ask help, advice, and to pray with him. He was persuaded to join a small community of monks at Vicovaro, becoming recognised as their abbot, but his strict rule was too difficult for them and they tried to get rid of him. They put poison into his cup of wine but, as he blessed the cup before drinking from it, the cup shattered into small pieces and Benedict's life was saved.

He left them to return to the mountains of Subiaco. On the summit there was an altar to the pagan god Appollo and it was here that Benedict destroyed the heathen altar and founded his monastic community. Starting with two small communities, he gradually increased the strength of the monastery until he had developed twelve separate establishments. Here he developed the monastic life for his followers. The love and patience of Benedict enabled him to work out a rule 'for beginners', as he put it, which covered all aspects of community life within a monastery. His 'little rule' concerned the inner spiritual life of the monk, the order of life and worship, reltionships between the members of the community and their contacts, and influence on the lay community outside.

The basis of Benedict's rule was the concept of the family with the abbot as father. The individual monk's life was set in love, courtesy and hospitality. This was the setting for God's work of regular praise and worship in word, psalm, song, biblical reading and prayer. There was hard work too, for the monastery had to be self-supporting and indeed become the centre of agricultural life for the community surrounding it. They became cultural centres amid a barbaric world. All this, because one young man set out to follow a religious life. Benedict broke down the prejudice that manual work was degrading and each monk was involved in every aspect of the community life. There is no doubt that he was a hard taskmaster, but not an unkind one.

A story is told that one young monk was hacking away at the undergrowth near a lake with a kind of hatchet when the metal head flew off into the water. He was very upset about this, fearing that Benedict would be angry. However, Benedict came upon the unfortunate monk and, when he heard what had happened, told the monk to throw the wooden handle into the water as well. Immediately, a hand appeared from the water bearing the wooden handle of the hatchet with the metal head firmly fixed to it. We cannot believe that this actually happened, but we must believe in Benedict's even greater miracle of blending together all the elements in those primitive communities and achieving such unity of purpose.

However, an envious priest called Florentius tried to upset Benedict's rule and he was helped by the fragmented nature of the twelve separate communities. Benedict realised that this was a personal thing and resolved to leave Subiaco and made his way to Monte Cassino, a solitary, elevated place with deep narrow ravines on three sides. Learning from his experience at Subiaco, he kept his new community as one and it was here that he perfected his 'rule'. His monastery was 'a school for the Lord's Service'. Monte Cassino became a focal point for visitors, lay and clerical. There was no shortage of monks who wanted to join this community which was to face desolation many times, the first by Lombard barbarians only forty years after its foundation.

Benedict's rule was written out formally by Pope Gregory some fifty years after his death, and his sister, Scholastica founded nunneries which followed much the same rule. Brother and sister died within weeks of each other.

His rule was, and still is, followed by Benedictine communities all over the world. In England, Benedictine monks were among the early missionaries, setting up houses in Canterbury, Westminster, Ely, Winchester, Fountains, Tintern and many other places. Monte Cassino, where Benedict lies buried, has been destroyed many times but always a new monastery rises on the site.

St Richard of Chichester   (b. 1197)   *3 April*

Richard was born at Wyche, an English town noted for its brine springs where well-to-do people went to 'take the waters'. Its modern name is Droitwich. His father could be considered a local squire, a land owner with a comfortable income. While Richard was quite young both his parents died and the steward in charge allowed the estate to run down through his neglect and laziness. As soon as Richard and his older brother realised what was happening and were old enough to do something about it, the steward was discharged and the sons set about retrieving the family fortune. Richard literally put his hand to the plough and, mostly due to his hard work, the estate prospered. The older brother, to show his gratitude, offered to make over the property to Richard and went so far as to find a wealthy young lady who should be Richard's wife. The brother repented of his generosity and in any case Richard would have found such a life unsatisfactory. He resigned to his brother both the estate and the young lady, left home and set out on a new life at Oxford University, knowing that he would have to live on a poor income. In spite of a lack of funds, he enjoyed the company of scholars and students; he loved learning and he found poverty no drawback. He was so poor that he had to share an academic gown with another student, taking turns at wearing it. Food was scarce and they could only afford a fire on special occasions. He had the good fortune to be at Oxford at a time when the university had a host of eminent scholars.

Among the many friends made by Richard was Edmund Rich, one of the great chancellors of the university. From Oxford, Richard went on to study in the universities in Paris and Bologna, achieving high academic success at these famous centres of medieval learning. Once again, he had the opportunity of marrying the daughter of a wealthy tutor, but Richard returned to Oxford to take his Master's degree and to occupy the Chancellor's chair.

During this period in our history the leaders of the church, wielding considerable power, often came into conflict with the king. The quarrel between Henry II and Thomas Becket is an example of this.

Henry III deliberately refused to make appointments in the church so that the income during a vacancy could be paid into the king's own resources. This meant that some parishes had to suffer long periods without a priest, and that a church diocese might have to carry on without a bishop. Richard and Edmund Rich argued long and wearily on this matter until the situation became unbearable and, when Edmund died, Richard left England to join a Dominican monastery in Orleans, France. There he took holy orders and became a priest. He returned to England to take up the modest post of a priest in Deal.

In the year 1244, the Bishop of Chichester died and the king appointed Robert Passelwee to this office. This was a man who by underhand means had added a considerable amount of money to the royal treasury. The archbishop considered him worthless and refused to confirm the appointment. The archbishop declared that he was prepared to appoint Richard. This, Henry refused and once more Richard left the country to plead his cause before the Pope in Rome. Henry was furious at this development, especially when he learned that the Pope consecrated Richard as Bishop of Chichester in a ceremony held in Rome.

Richard came back to England to take up his office but, on his return, found that the king had forbidden anyone to give him money or houseroom; the gates of the bishop's palace were locked so that Richard could not get in, and the people of Chichester were too frightened to help him.

For two years, Richard wandered about the diocese of Chichester, holding meetings, conducting services, and generally living a most uncomfortable life, existing on the charity of the few people who dared to defy the king. One kindly priest, Simon of Tarry, gave Richard shelter in his own home.

The Pope then intervened and declared that he would excommunicate the king if he did not allow Richard to take up his post as Bishop of Chichester. This was a terrible threat in those days and Henry gave in.

Richard was enthroned and could now do his job as bishop properly. He was generous in his hospitality to visitors but lived austerely himself. He wore plain clothing over a hair shirt, which must have been very uncomfortable. He won the affection of all his people by the simplicity of his life and the standards he set in Christian principles and virtues. He gave up all his earthly possessions to the church. On one occasion when money was needed to support the poor, he ordered the steward to sell some gold and silver dishes. The steward objected but Richard was firm, adding, 'There is my horse too. He should fetch a good price'.

Richard set out on a strenuous campaign of preaching along the south coast, giving no thought for himself, or even for his health. He caught a fever that was to be fatal. He was carried to a house of poor priests, called Maison Dieu at Dover, where he died. Only the day before, ill as he was, he had consecrated a church in honour of his former master, St Edmund.

St Bernadette   (b. 1844)   *16 April*

Nobody who knew Marie Bernadette Sobirous as a child could ever have believed that she was destined to be one of the most popular saints of all time. Her father eked out a poor living as a miller in Lourdes, a town in southern France. He worked long hours for poor money in order to keep his large family from starving. Bernadette was his eldest child, and those who knew her considered her dull but nevertheless had a pleasant manner in her contacts with adults and other children. The Soubirous family was devout in its religious observance and Bernadette was a good child. From the first she was a delicate girl, afflicted with asthma and other ailments inevitable from living in the dark, damp and airless basement of a dilapidated house. She suffered, too, from the effects of a cholera epidemic.

One day, when she was fourteen years old, she went to play and pick flowers along the banks of the nearby river. She came to a shallow cave and, as she stood in the entrance, she saw a lady who talked with her and indicated the presence of a long-forgotten spring of clear fresh water which from that moment began to flow again. The lady told Bernadette that she was Mary, the Mother of Jesus. Bernadette first saw the vision on 11 February, 1858, and during the following weeks she claimed that she saw Mary on eighteen occasions. Sometimes other children or grown-ups went with her, but they could see nothing unusual. Yet they heard Bernadette talking earnestly as if someone else was there. There seemed to be no doubt that Bernadette saw and heard something. Naturally, the people of Lourdes were half disbelieving and half frightened by this strange occurrence and at first said that Bernadette must be deranged, silly or insane. Of course the local priest and the local doctor talked to her and examined her. They could find nothing strange about Bernadette, physically, mentally, or emotionally but such was the insistence of Bernadette that she had seen and talked to the Mother of Jesus that the Roman Catholic Church authorities felt that they had to investigate the strange experience which Bernadette had described. The story of Bernadette's vision spread rapidly and people began to come to Lourdes to see the girl, and more particularly to visit the spot where Mary had appeared to her.

It was impossible for Bernadette to live a normal life and she suffered agonies both from those who said she had made the story up and was a cheat, and from those who held her up as a visionary and saintly character. It was a strange ordeal for this girl who, even when she was eighteen, was no more mature than a child. She was bewildered when people asked her to bless them, to cut pieces from her clothes, to question her at all hours of the day and the night. She wanted no reward for all this but often wanted to be alone. One priest who seemed to imagine that he was favouring her, persuaded her to give him her rosary, for which she would take no money. She was wearing a scapular, which is worn across the shoulders as part of the dress, indicating her membership of a religious order. It was made of two rectangles of material joined by strings. The priest asked her to cut it in two so that he should have half. 'No,' said Bernadette, 'Would you give me back half of the rosary I gave you?' 'Of course not,' said the priest. 'Then I cannot divide my scapular.' This is said to be the nearest she ever got to being irritated by her questioners.

She was never well but as she suffered from all the visitors who wanted to meet her, talk to her and question her, she was admitted to a convent. By now she was very ill with severe asthma. In 1876 a great church was built near the spot where Bernadette had seen the Mother of Jesus but she did not attend the ceremony at which the church was consecrated and opened to all. The pressure of people on her would have been too much. 'If only I could go to see and not be seen,' she said.

When she was very ill one of the sisters asked her about her former fame and enquired how she felt now that she was not in the public eye. She replied that she was like a broom. 'Our Lady used me and now I am put back in the corner.'

She died when she was thirty-five years old but that was far from the last that the world heard of her. Visitors who came with illness and disease to the spring which flowed from the hollow cave began to find that their visits made them better and many declared that they had been cured.

The Roman Catholic Church does not easily give credit for such things and eminent doctors were employed to investigate their claims. Many were false, or could easily be put down to natural causes. Even so, some of the cures could not be so easily explained and in time there was a long list of cures that could only be called miraculous. After long and searching investigation, it seemed to the Church Authorities that many such cures could only be attributed to the intervention of Bernadette.

In due course, the Church declared her a saint. She was nominated St Mary Bernadette, but the world knows her as St Bernadette of Lourdes.

Many pilgrims still visit Lourdes, some just curious to see the place where she claimed to have seen Mary, the Mother of Jesus, some to be inspired by being present at the place where she lived, some hoping to be cured of illness, some finding a spiritual strength from visiting the spot where Mary showed herself to a poor, sick girl, whose name was to be known all over the world.

St Anselm   (b. 1033)   *21 April*

Every pupil in the schools of Britain must surely know the date of the Norman landing and victory at the Battle of Hastings. (If not, there is a hilarious book called *1066 and all that* which comments on our history in a light-hearted way.) One of the advantages of that conquest was that two great leaders of Church and State successively occupied the post of Archbishop of Canterbury. The first was Lanfranc, and the second was his successor at Canterbury, Anselm.

Anselm was born at Aosta in Italy, the son of a Lombard nobleman. From an early age he had a feeling for the life of a monk and, when he was about fifteen years old, he presented himself to a monastery. The abbot questioned him closely and declared that he did not consider Anselm fitted for such a life and refused to accept him. This rebuff upset Anselm and his reaction was to turn right away from a religious life and to live in a completely selfish way. He became high-spirited, made friends with very wordly people and lived in a way that many described as wicked. Then, when he was about twenty-six years old, his mode of life changed again. He was then at Bec, in northern France, where he found a monastery and his former urge to become a monk returned. The prior who interviewed him was Lanfranc, who saw beneath the appearance of this apparently frivolous man and accepted him.

In three years he had so impressed the other monks by his devotion and selfless life that when Lanfranc left to become abbot of a larger, more important community, the monks of Bec elected Anselm as their prior, a senior post next to the abbot. Of course, some of the older monks who had been passed over were upset and disappointed but Anselm won them over, including a young man named Osborn who, unfortunately, fell ill and was nursed by Anselm until his early death.

Anselm was strict in his control of the younger monks, yet introduced modern methods of education in their training, allowing considerable freedom of thought.

Fifteen years later, Anselm became abbot. During the thirty years or so that he served at the monastery at Bec, Anselm wrote many books on philosophy and theology that were so important that he was called 'the Father of Scholasticism'. He encouraged argument and questioning rather than blind obedience from his monks. 'If you plant a tree and bind it on all sides so that the branches will not spread out, what sort of tree will it be when in later years you gave it room to spread? Yet that is how children are often treated in their learning, debarring them from the enjoyment of freedom.'

As abbot, Anselm had to travel, often coming to England where his former friend and teacher, Lanfranc, was now Archbishop of Canterbuy, and he happened to be in England when Lanfranc died. The Pope nominated Anselm as the new Archbishop of Canterbury but the king, who insisted that he should have the right to appoint to this important post, decided not to agree to the appointment of Anselm so that he, the king, could take all the rents, revenues and income, which the archbishop should use in the management of the church. William is said to have declared, 'By the holy face of Lucca (a favourite oath of the king) Anselm nor anyone else will be

Archbishop of Canterbury as long as I live.' Soon after this the king fell ill and, fearing that he might die, agreed to the appointment. As soon as he was well again, William Rufus returned to his old ways, diverting money that was not his into the royal coffers. There followed a long quarrel between them, with churchmen and barons taking sides. Eventually things went against Anselm and he had to leave, travelling to Rome so that he could report to the Pope exactly what was happening in England.

The death of William Rufus meant that Anselm could come back but almost immediately he was involved in the same sort of arguments with the new king, Henry I. Once more Anselm was sent into exile and the king claimed all the revenues that should have gone to the church. With the help of the Pope, a settlement was achieved and Anselm came back to Canterbury, with a great deal of rejoicing by the clergy and the people. But all these journeys and quarrels had had an effect on Anselm's health and he died in 1109 at Canterbury in the midst of his own friends, the monks.

Anselm was a fine man, with great sympathy for poor people and those in difficulties. He was one of the first to oppose slavery, although it was to be many centuries before slavery in this country was abolished. He loved God's creatures and a story is told of him coming across a boy who had tied a string to bird's leg to keep it captive. Anselm cut the thread and said, 'The bird flies away; the boy cries; God is glad.'

St George (b. *c.*300) 23 April

The flag of St George, a red cross on a white background, is the correct flag for churches to fly on great occasions in the Church's year or on national days. There are about 150 churches dedicated to him, scores of hostelries which bear his name and almost every town of any size has a George Street. In spite of this, who he was and how exactly he became the patron saint of England are both uncertain.

The probability is that George was a young soldier serving

the Emperor of Rome in his native area of Lydda. Another version of the story places him in Cappadocia. He had been converted and baptised into the Christian faith, although in his day it was wise not to make such a fact too obvious. There had been during his youth a quiet period when the Roman authority was tolerant of this relatively new faith, but the Emperor Diocletion broke this period of tolerance by proclaiming a new persecution of Christian believers. They were to be tortured and, if in defiance of this, they continued to hold their belief they should be put to death.

George was seen tearing down one of these hateful notices and was quickly reported to the authority. He was arrested, tortured and finally put to death for his belief. That is all there is to the story of George. But, what about the dragon?

The stories about George and the Dragon were added very much later, probably five or six hundred years later. During the Middle Ages it was common to make up stories about the heroes and heroines to increase faith. The excuse must have been that, while it was not at all certain that these heroic people actually did the deeds attributed to them, they were the sort of people who could have acted so.

The fullest version of the legend of St George is to be found in *Legenda Aurea* by the Blessed James of Varaigne, translated and printed by William Caxton.

George was a Christian knight who in his travels came on a city called Sylene, which adjoined a vast swampland. Within the swamps lived a dragon which 'envenomed the whole land'. Many times the citizens joined forces to kill it when it emerged from the swamps but its breath was so terrible that they fled before it. To placate the dragon the townsfolk offered their sheep, but as their flocks dwindled and eventually died out, the dragon demanded human sacrifice. Victims were selected by lottery and eventually the lot fell to the king's own daughter. She dressed herself in white, like a bride, and went forth bravely to satisfy the monster. Providentially, George was passing by on horseback and, riding before her, he attacked the dragon and after fearful, bloody battle, George transfixed it with a thrust of his lance. The creature was not dead but suffered the young girl to encircle its neck with the white cord from round her waist and, leading the defeated dragon, George and the princess re-entered the city. 'It followed her as if it had been a meek beast and debonair'. The citizens emerged from their hiding places and declared George a hero. He promised that if they would embrace the Christian faith, he would destroy the dragon. This he did with a final thrust of his lance and the body of the creature was drawn away on four ox carts to be lost in the swamplands for ever. The account tells us that 'there were about 15,000 men baptised, not counting the women and children'. The king offered George great treasures but George insisted that the money should be distributed among the poor. He left the town with four behests:

1. The king should maintain the churches.
2. The king should honour priests.
3. The king should attend church services.
4. The king should show compassion for the poor.

The story has been repeatedly embellished from time to time. But what has this to do with England? Bede, in his history, mentions George, and even in Norman times the story was known in England. It appears that during one of the early Crusades, when the English Crusaders were doing badly, George appeared to the soliders and encouraged them to fight harder until they overcame the Turks. Then Richard 'the Lion Heart' saw the opportunity of encouraging his troops by accepting George as their patron and encouraged the soldiers to paint St George's red cross on their shields.

Until then, Edward the Confessor had been England's patron, but in 1222, St George's Day was declared a national holiday and St George became England's patron saint. Edward III later founded the Order of the Knights of St George, or the Order of the Garter. St George was accepted and at one time the feast day of the patron saint was celebrated as enthusiastically as Christmas.

The emblem of that almost unknown Roman soldier flies above the great majority of English churches and one of the most famous lines of Shakespeare, from *Henry V*, evokes patriotic sentiment: 'Cry God for Harry, England and St George'.

St Mark   (1st Century)   *25 April*

It must be admitted that we do not know a great deal about Mark, even though one of the four gospels in the Bible is attributed to him.

The evidence of the gospels indicates that a householder in Jerusalem named Mary had a son, John, surnamed Mark, and it seems likely that Jesus and his followers used to meet at this house. Assuming that this is true, then Jesus and his disciples met at this house on the night before His trial and Crucifixion. When they left the house to walk to the garden of Gethsemane, the young boy, Mark, got out of bed, flung a blanket round his shoulders and followed them. He witnessed the betrayal of Jesus by Judas with a kiss, the anger of Peter who took a sword and cut off a man's ear, and the arrest of Jesus by the soldiers. One of the soldiers saw this young lad and ran to catch him. Mark ran away but the soldier was faster and, catching up with the boy, took hold of the blanket. Mark freed himself from the blanket and ran off home, naked.

When he grew older, Mark became a friend and follower of Paul, setting out with him and Barnabas on Paul's first missionary journey. In the gospels, Mark is referred to as a kinsman of Barnabas and it is most likely that they were both Levites, men who assisted the priests in the ceremonies in the Jewish Temple. This missionary journey was to Cyprus, but it seems that Paul was not convinced of Mark's steadfastness and he was left out of the second mission to Asia Minor. There is an account of Mark's assistancce to Paul when he was taken captive in Rome. Having been reconciled with Paul, Mark lived in Rome where he wrote his gospel. The rest of his life was probably spent in Alexandria.

Tradition also links Mark with Peter, for in one of his letters from Rome Peter refers to 'my son Mark'. One account indicates that Mark became Bishop of Alexandria and that, after preaching there, he was arrested, bound with cords, and grievously tortured. He died as a result of these experiences. In fact, we do not know for certain how Mark died but the city of Venice has always proclaimed Mark as its patron saint and also claims that Mark's body is buried beneath the great chapel of the Doges — the dukes of Venice.

Many legends associate Mark with Venice. The most common story is that Venetian merchants stole the body of Mark from the infidels of Alexandria. The body was then carried by boat, beneath piles of pork meat, which Muslim customs men would not handle. Another story tells us that the body was lost in a great fire in the Basilica but returned miraculously, bursting out of a stone pillar.

The great chapel today, more like a cathedral to its teeming visitors, is dedicated to St Mark and the immense square in front of the chapel is St Mark's Square, or Piazza. The emblem of Mark, a winged lion, can be seen everywhere in Venice, in carvings, in stone, in paintings, but nowhere so nobly as surmounting a pillar overlooking the lagoon.

St Dunstan (b. *c.*924)   *19 May*

It can well be claimed that Dunstan is the most famous of the Anglo-Saxon saints. It was Dunstan who instituted and indeed ruled that all monasteries should follow the custom of ringing bells to mark celebrations of services, and to ring even longer peals on special occasions. Due to his insistence, religious and national functions were marked by bell ringing. Dunstan, together with his friend and colleague Bishop Ethelwold, cast two of the bells for Abingdon monastery. It is also due to Dunstan that the making and playing of organs in church ceremonial and worship was revived after they had ceased to be made for nearly a century before he was born.

Dunstan was born in Glastonbury in Somerset. He was of noble birth, related to the royal household, and he was soon recognised as having a brilliant brain, excelling in everything that he attempted. He was educated by Irish scholars at Glastonbury and, when he was quite young, was appointed to a place in the household of King Athelston. It is not surprising to learn that other boys, jealous of his intellectual power, told lies about him and played tricks on him to such an extent that their torment made him ill and he had to leave the court. He suffered from fevers, and bouts of sleepwalking which were not understood in those days. He himself thought he had leprosy. He was urged to become a priest and, after taking holy orders, returned to Glastonbury and lived a quieter life in a small rough cell within the monastery.

His interests and skills developed in every direction. Of course, he spent much of his time in prayer and in the regular service of the Christian community, but he also read innumerable books, made bells and sacred vessels from metal, copied and illustrated books, played a harp, wrote music, and designed embroideries for the church.

When Athelston died, Dunstan fell out of favour, for the next king, Edmund, was envious of Dunstan's ability and refused his presence at the royal court. However, while he was out hunting, King Edmund, chasing a stag above Cheddar Gorge, was nearly tossed over the edge of a precipice. Realising his danger, the king cried out that he would restore Dunstan if he were to be saved. The horse came to a stop at the very edge of the cliff and the king's life was saved.

Dunstan was eventually made Abbot of Glastonbury and from then on the religious life of England was given new strength. The period of the Danish invasions had been bad for the church but now Dunstan encouraged new monastic building, restoration of churches, founding libraries and raising the standard of people's service to the church and to God.

King Edmund was succeeded by his son, Edred, who admired Dunstan but, sadly, died young. His successor, a nephew named Edwig, was not at all religious, spending his time in gaming and frivolous pursuits. When Dunstan dared to rebuke him, the new king banished Dunstan from the country.

This was a blessing in disguise for Dunstan travelled to France where he saw a well-ordered, disciplined monastery at work. This was a wonderful experience for him and, on his recall to England by Edwig's successor, Edward, he came back full of ideas for improving the Christian life in the monasteries, and in the church. He had experienced the full flowering of the monastic rule established by Benedict.

Dunstan was appointed Bishop of Worcester and then

Archbishop of Canterbury, and his encouragement of the monastic life and his influence on it lasted until the time when Henry VIII, nearly five hundred years later, crushed the monasteries, bringing about their dissolution.

Dunstan did not see monks as being isolated in a monastery but as taking a positive role in church and national life. Dunstan also worked towards conciliation and friendship with the Danes. Unfortunately, Edward was succeeded by Ethelred, rather an ineffective king, nicknamed 'the unready'.

Dunstan was a firm educationalist and loved to teach the scholars in his cathedral school. Long after his death the school used a prayer which invoked the help of 'their sweet Father Dunstan'.

Dunstan retired from public life as, although only sixty-four years old, he was near the end of his life. On Ascension Day he celebrated his last service. He preached to his people three times during the service and later said that Jesus appeared to him. He asked the people to pray for him for he was soon to die. He returned to his cathedral, chose his burial place, and died two days later.

Dunstan is the patron saint of goldsmiths, jewellers and locksmiths. His skill as a metal worker gave rise to the story that once when the Devil appeared before him in order to tempt him into evil, Dunstan took a pair of blacksmith's tweezers and seized the Devil's nose in them; thus the Devil's nose was put out of joint!

St Augustine   (b. *c*.605)   *26 May*

Canterbury is synonymous with the Church of England, for the Archbishop of Canterbury is the highest authority in the Church. Augustine was the first to hold that title but we know little about him in his youth. He was a young, enthusiastic and eloquent prior of St Andrew's Monastery in Rome at the time when Gregory was Pope. The story goes that Gregory, passing through the streets of Rome, saw some young fair-haired boys and men being offered for sale as slaves, or servants, in the market place. It was customary for the Roman army to take captives from among the people in lands occupied by the Romans and offer them in the market to work in the households of wealthy Romans. Their fair skin and hair was impressive among the dark Italians and the Pope was impelled to stop and ask who these people were. He was told that they were Angles. 'Surely not Angles, but Angels,' he said wittily. 'Where do they come from?' he next asked. 'From Deira, in northern Britain,' was the reply. 'Then we must save them from the wrath (*de ira*) of God.' Finally, he asked who ruled their land. He was told that their king was Aella. 'Then we shall see to it that Alleluia shall be sung in that land.' There was already a Christian influence in Britain, brought by great men like Cedd, Chad, Aidan and others, but the southern part of England was less affected.

Pope Gregory chose Augustine to head a mission to the southern part of England and he, with about thirty other monks, set out for England. However, most of Augustine's companions heard terrifying stories about the barbarians they would meet and the great dangers faced by those who ventured into England. They turned back and Augustine had to report to Pope Gregory that he had failed. Gregory once more inspired Augustine to set out again and in fact promoted him to become abbot. The monks found that the perils they had to face had been exaggerated and they landed safely in Kent where the king, Ethelbert, already knew something of the Christian faith. Although he was not Christian, his wife Bertha was, and persuaded her husband to let her retain her own bishop.

The king arranged to meet Augustine in a field at Ebbsfleet and it must have been a magnificent sight when Augustine and his monks, robed and bearing banners, came in procession to meet him. He preached to the king who then gave him permission to live in Canterbury and make converts, all at the king's expense.

The Christians used an existing church, St Martin's, as their base and went about preaching, teaching and healing. Ethelbert was so impressed with the Christians that in the year 597 at Whitsuntide he was himself baptised. During a visit to

France, Augustine was consecrated 'Bishop of the English'. The following Christmas about 10,000 men of Kent with their families were baptised into the Christian faith.

Augustine sent two monks to Rome to ask for more help in his successful campaign and was rewarded with gifts of 'all things needed in general worship and the service of the church', to use the Pope's expression. These included altar vessels, furnishings, vestments, relics and books.

Pope Gregory outlined for Augustine the course he should take. He insisted that pagan temples should not be destroyed but converted to Christian churches. Local holidays and customs should not be abolished but retained and overlaid with Christian emphasis. The holidays would indeed be Holy Days, celebrating the great Christian festivals and honouring the saints. It is not surprising that when we examine our great festivals today we find pagan symbolism. Mistletoe and holly at Christmas, eggs at Easter and so on, are all reminders of our pagan past. Indeed the very name Easter derives from the name of a pagan god and, in itself, has no Christian derivation. Gregory excused this attitude in the words, 'He who would climb to a lofty height must go by steps — not leaps.'

Yet, in Britain, there was a clear division in practice between the Christians of the eastern half of England and those who had been driven west into Cornwall and Wales, and north into parts of Scotland by the Viking invasions. There were differences in practice and belief, finding a focal point in the reckoning of the date of Easter.

Augustine made many overtures to the leaders of the western churches, without success. The breaking point came when Augustine invited his opposite numbers to meet at a place now known as Augustine's Oak. Unfortunately, as the western church leaders approached, Augustine failed to stand to meet them. This was sufficient to create ill-feeling and the opportunity for reconciliation was lost.

Maybe that is why, even today, when there is greater unity in the Church, Augustine's feast day in England is May 26, but elsewhere it is May 28.

St Bede   (b. 673)

The Venerable Bede was born in Northumbria in a village not far from Jarrow, and spent his whole life in that part of England, never going any further afield than Lindisfarne and York. Most of his life was spent within the enclosed walls of a monastery. He wrote many works, but is best known for his *History of the English Church and People*. He is perhaps the best known personality and writer of his time and is recognised as the one who has given us most understanding of that period. His history is still a classic, used by researchers and historians even today. He was so modest that he said that he would not mind if nobody ever read his work since he found his own enjoyment and spiritual development was sufficient reason for his writing.

At the age of seven, Bede entered the monastery at Wearmouth, then a year later he transferred to Jarrow where he spent the rest of his life, until he was fifty-five years old. Although it was well within his reach, he never became Abbot of Jarrow, largely because he felt unworthy of such high office.

To those of us used to living in modern communities with opportunities of meeting different people, joining in all sorts of community activities with the busy world about us, the thought of living one's whole life within the bounds of a monastery, with its rigid rules and disciplines, seems stifling and crippling. What is it like to be a monk in a closed order?

First, there is the discipline of regular worship throughout every day; the routine of attending services, chanting psalms, joining in prayer, participating in the ritual and making one's own prayers during the silent moments. The monastic life affords plenty of opportunity for reflecting on one's beliefs, inadequacies, triumphs and expectations, while also praying for other people.

This worship alternates between writing, reading and personal thought and prayer, with the daily tasks dictated by the life of the community. Here, each monk has his own skill to contribute. There is work in the kitchens, the bakery, the smithy, on the farm, in making furniture, furnishings and other articles for the comfort of all. Some private time is allotted for exercise and writing, or any other art or craft which any member wishes to develop. Of course, each monk has a room, or cell, and of necessity some part of the twenty-four day is spent in sleep. Sometimes a monk falls ill, so there has to be a hospital wing with those in charge who are experienced doctors.

Meals are eaten together in accordance with the rules of the order; often these are taken in silence while one member reads aloud. Visitors are welcome and the community keeps abreast of the events in the world. It all sounds rather dull and monotous but there is a lot of fun and life is not always solemn and serious.

The centre of monastic life is, of course, the church and monks become accomplished musicians and singers. It was at Bede's monastery that Gregorian chanting was first introduced. Monks sometimes misbehaved and occasionally missed services, but Bede was noted for his regularity. On one occasion when the monastery at Jarrow suffered a plague and almost all the monks either died or were seriously ill, the services were continued with only the abbot and young Bede attending.

Monks are not necessarily priests of the church and Bede was not ordained until he was thirty. Jarrow had a school and Bede was soon recognised as a great teacher, one of his pupils later becoming Archbishop of York, who founded a similar school there.

Bede was in the process of translating St John's gospel into English for his students when he fell ill, finding breathing difficult. He continued to teach and write from his bed. When he was too weak to write he began to dictate from his bed. On the day before Ascension Day, a major festival of the church, he was very ill indeed. One of his pupils said, 'Master, there is still one chapter to do. Is it too troublesome to go on?' 'No,' said Bede, 'take your pen and write faster.' He grew tired during the afternoon and sent for his brother monks to give them gifts. The pupil said, 'Master, there is still a little more to do.' He said, 'Write quickly.' After a moment or two the pupil said, 'It is finished.' The saint said a short prayer and died.

He was buried at Jarrow but his body was later removed to Durham and in Henry II's reign he was laid to rest in the Galilee Chapel at the west end of the cathedral.

The title 'Venerable' was a term of respect bestowed on distinguished members of holy orders. It was conferred on Bede at one of the great councils of the church in Aachen held in 836. St Boniface said of Bede that he was a 'light of the Church lit by the Holy Ghost.'

St Joan   (b. 1412)   *30 May*

Now that the story of this young girl who lived for less than twenty years in the fifteenth century is so well known, it is difficult to understand why the Catholic church took nearly 500 years to decide that she was worthy to be declared a saint. Another young French girl, Teresa of Lisieux, whose story you will find elsewhere in this book, was declared a saint only twenty-eight years after her death.

However, Joan the Maid, or Jeanne La Pucelle, better known as Joan of Arc in England, was born in a little village in Normandy during the confusing days of the early fifteenth century when both England and France were seeking to bind opposing elements and interests within themselves and to assert supremacy over the other. Charles was the King of France but was not yet crowned, being known as the Dauphin, rather like the English title of Prince of Wales. Neither he nor Henry V of England could be certain of authority in his own country but could increase his power by asserting the right to rule over the other's country. Indeed, Charles was fighting not only the English but the Burgundians who, although French, had joined forces with Henry of England because they thought it would pay them to do so. Charles was unfortunately no soldier and was despised by his own followers.

Joan, a country girl of about fourteen, only vaguely understood the political situation, but she was a patriotic girl and was certain that the English could be thrown back. She was devout and prayed regularly for the safety of France.

Through her prayers she heard the 'voices' of the saints telling her that she would be the saviour of her country. These manifestations first seemed to be a single voice coming from within a blaze of light. Gradually the number of voices increased and Joan seemed able to identify them as belonging to various saints. Her friends and family in the village were astonished at this, but she left the village and insisted that the commander of the local garrison should provide her with soldier's clothes, a horse and an escort to help her find her way into the court of the Dauphin in Chinon. The commander, Robert Beaudricourt, at first refused but changed his mind when official confirmation came of a French defeat that Joan had foretold.

She so impressed those who met her that she was eventually brought to Charles and persuaded him to let her join the commander of the French Army, Dunois. At that time, half of the French army was beseiged by the English in Orleans, while Dunois held the remainder of the French on the opposite bank of the River Loire. Dunois had rafts prepared to take his forces across the river to beat back the English, recapture the town and allow the French forces to link up again. His problem was that the wind was blowing strongly against him and until it changed the rafts loaded with soldiers could not cross. Joan told Dunois that the answer was simple. They had to ask God to change the direction of the wind. She left him to go to pray in the local church. When she got back to Dunois the wind had changed and she was one of the first to cross the river and inspire the French to defeat the English.

The French army that had been so dejected now found new heart and the Maid led them to two further victories over the English. Charles entered Rheims and was crowned King of France, with Joan at his side. Through all these events the French marvelled at Joan's bravery and skill, but were even more impressed by her simple faith in God to whom she attributed all her successes. But success inevitably breeds jealousy in others, even on the part of so-called friends. When they had a chance, the Burgundians captured Joan and sold her to the English, who imprisoned her while they schemed how she could be put to death.

For nine long months she remained in prison, brutally treated but constant in her life of prayer and service to God. A court of churchmen was appointed, not so much for their fairness but for their unscrupulous service to the English authority. She was accused of witchcraft and heresy, being urged to confess that her 'voices' came from the Devil and not from God. She endured fifteen sessions at the hands of this court, but she never wavered from her insistence that she was a devout daughter of the church and that her inspiration was from God.

For a brief moment she almost gave way, but when she learned that even so her judges would send her to solitary confinement in a prison cell for the rest of her life, she declared that this proved to her that their judgement was from the Devil and that her 'voices' were from God. She was handed over to the English soldiers and burned to death in the market place of Rouen. As the flames mounted round her she asked for a cross. An English soldier tied together two rough pieces of wood and handed it up to her. She died in the flames holding the crude cross before her eyes.

After her death her ashes were cast into the River Seine and one of King Henry's secretaries, John Tressart, was heard to cry, 'We are lost, we have burned a saint.'

It was in 1456 that Pope Callistus appointed a commission which found that her sentence had been obtained by fraud and deceit and that she was a true child of God, but it took another four and a half centuries to decide that she was saint.

St Boniface (b. c.675)   *5 June*

Boniface, born in Credition in Devon about the year 675, was destined to become one of the most notable sons of the county. Coming from a rich and noble family, possibly the most outstanding personality in northern Europe of his time, yet he chose a simple, single-hearted way of life that was to take him to a martyr's death.

He was christened Winfrid. He would sit quietly listening to the many visitors to his family household, recognising that many of them were monks. By the time he was four years old he had made up his mind that he too would take the vows and become a monk himself. Two years later he became a pupil at a monastic school near Exeter. He was a pupil of Wimbert and was influenced by the great Aldhelm, himself destined to become a saint. Winfrid became director of the monastery school but he always felt that his calling was to wider fields of missionary work. He was a skilled teacher with a personal popularity that attracted students to him. His notes were copied and circulated for many students who could not get to hear him personally. He compiled the first book of Latin grammar to be used in English schools. However, Winfrid was thirty-six years old before his abbot gave him permission to leave the monastery. His first missionary efforts in Holland were not successful, for the social and political conditions in that part of Europe were unfavourable.

He appreciated that to achieve greater success he needed the patronage of the Pope and, to obtain this, he journeyed to Rome to seek the help of Gregory II. The Pope advised him to change his name to Boniface and to turn his attention to Saxony, in central Germany. For the next twenty years he spread the Christian faith over many parts of Europe, even finding success in Holland where before he had failed. He was created bishop, and his work included preaching, converting the pagans, organising and founding monasteries as well as repairing churches burnt or damaged by heathens, who were infuriated by his successes in converting so many of their people to Christianity.

After the death of a pagan ruler, Radbod, who had opposed Boniface, there opened up even greater prospects of success. He came to be known as the 'Apostle of Germany' and to him goes much of the credit for evangelizing and civilizing the great regions of central Germany. Christopher Dawson, an English historian, wrote that 'Boniface had a deeper influence on the history of Europe than any Englishman who has ever lived.'

There are many legends connected with Boniface but perhaps the most famous is about his meeting with the heathen

worshippers of the pagan god, Thor. This god was particularly
venerated at the spot where a great oak tree was standing.
Boniface confronted the heathen worshippers by this oak and
declared that he was going to chop it down. The heathen
people were outraged and called on Thor to strike down this
man. Boniface took an axe and cut away at the tree. Possibly
because a favourable wind was blowing, the tree crashed to the
ground, split into four parts and Boniface was unharmed. This
act brought many converts over to Christianity and on the spot
where the tree had stood, Boniface built a church in honour of
St Peter. Sadly, Boniface never saw England again although it
is evident that England and her people were ever in his
thoughts and prayers.

Boniface by now was an important European personality, an
archbishop, and a friend and adviser of kings like Charles
Martel and Pepin. He could well have ended his days
surrounded by all that influence and riches could bring to him
but he preferred to remain faithful to the work he loved doing
most, that of a simple missionary.

When he was seventy-five he set out on a further mission to
Holland, where he had started his work as a missionary. He
took about fifty companions and carried a copy of the Gospels
and a book written by St Ambrose, entitled ominously 'Of a
good death'. The people of Friesland, who had previously
treated him so badly, now flocked round him to be converted
and baptised as Christians.

On Whit Sunday in the year 755, Boniface was to baptise
and confirm hundreds of converts. Sadly, the missionary camp
was invaded by hordes of savage fighters who came to avenge
their pagan gods. Boniface forbade his Christians to fight back.
'Children,' he said, 'let us not return evil for evil. Do not be
afraid of those who come to kill your body, but put your trust
in God who will receive you into His kingdom.' Some ran
away, but most stayed to die with Boniface. There is still
shown at Fulda the blood-stained Bible of Boniface. Perhaps
he laid his head on it as he awaited a death blow, or held it to
him as the sword thrusts pierced his body. In the raid in which
Boniface died the barbarians found nothing which seemed of

value to them. The items were mostly books, which they threw into the marshes.

Cuthbert, Archbishop of Canterbury, said, 'We, in England, lovingly count him one of the best and greatest leaders of the true faith.' An image of St Boniface can be seen on the front of Exeter Cathedral, but it is in Germany that one finds most statues, pictures and frescoes of him.

St William of York (b. *c*.1120) *8 June*

As a youth William was a lazy, pleasure-loving young man, not at all like the sort of person we usually visualise as likely to be numbered eventually among the saints of the Christian Church.

He was known as William FitzHerbert, or William of Thwayt, son of Emma, half-sister to the king of England, Stephen. He therefore had all the advantages of noble birth and good living. He was inevitably popular but lazy and when he was quite young, through the influence of his family, he was appointed treasurer to the churches of York. When, at the age of about twenty, he was appointed to the highly paid position of Archbishop of York, there was immediate bitter dispute and accusations of simony. (the undue influence of wealthy, well-connected people, including the king himself) and claims of unsuitability because of William's way of life.

However, King Stephen insisted on giving to William all the income and advantages of the office of archbishop, while Theobald, the Archbishop of Canterbury, hesitated to perform the ceremony of consecration. So, in a sense, William was, yet he wasn't Archbishop of York. The case was referred to the Pope in Rome who decided that he would support William if the Dean of York, another very important officer of the church, would swear on oath that there had been no undue influence. William was installed as archbishop but his enemies waited for a chance, which they were sure would come, to be rid of him. Surprisingly, William governed well, keeping good order as well as he could, but his easy-going way led to a disastrous oversight which played into his opponents' hands.

Now the Archbishop was not reckoned to be fully installed until he has received a pallium from the Pope. The pallium is one of the church robes, rather like an apron except that it hangs down both back and front. William's mistake was that he did not make arrangements for this ceremony and his enemies at once declared that they could not accept him as archbishop. This omission may not sound very important to us but it worried William who soon made his way to Rome. Here he found that the Pope had been given reports about his conduct which made him hesitate to confirm William's appointment. William, fearing to return to England, sought refuge with the King of Sicily. Back in England, William's supporters went on a rampage and burnt down Fountains Abbey. They desolated the farms around the abbey and assaulted Archdeacon Walter who had opposed William.

William returned to England and, to everyone's surprise, was a changed man. He now turned his back on all the luxurious living that he had enjoyed before and proved that he could be a model priest. He no longer moved in the extravagant circle of his former friends and gave all his time to religious observance and duties. He made his home with his uncle, Henry of Winchester, and lived an austere and penitential life in the monastery of that town. He kept to this style of life for six years, when the Archbishop of York died. William went to Rome once more where Pope Anastasius IV granted William's petition to be appointed to that office. From then on he was an exemplary character and the people of York eagerly awaited his return.

In May, 1154, he entered York once more and the crowd that gathered to welcome him was so vast that the weight of numbers on the wooden bridge which crossed the River Ouse caused the bridge to collapse, hurling scores of people into the water. Happily all who were thrown into the water were rescued and unhurt. This was attributed to the prayers of the restored Archbishop.

One of William's first acts was to visit Fountains Abbey and promise to restore it, wiping out the memory of all the destruction caused by his supporters some years before. However, he was not to see his promises put into effect, for only one month after his return to York he fell ill while celebrating Mass in the Cathedral. He suffered violent pains and within a few days he was dead. There was a rumour that one of his former enemies had poisoned him, but this was never proved.

In 1284 the body of William, which had been buried in a side chapel, was moved to the centre of the cathedral, a place of great honour.

His chief memorial at York is in one of the celebrated 'walls of glass' where many of the incidents in William's life are depicted, together with illustrations of some of his miracles.

St Columba   (b. *c.*521)   *9 June*

In the words of Bede, 'Columba, distinguished by his monastic habit and life, came from Ireland to Britain to preach the word of God in the provinces of the Northern Picts'. This most famous of Scottish saints was indeed an Irishman. Columba was one of those fortunate people who seem to have been blessed at birth with every advantage. His family was wealthy, influential and of noble descent. Columba himself was to become tall and good looking with a greatly impressive presence. He had intelligence, the advantage of good education, and was endowed with the skills of writer and artist and showed highly sensitive feeling for people and places.

He was born in 521 on the 7 December, in Donegal, Ireland, of the clan or family of O'Donell. With all his talent he could have become famous in almost any field of human activity. He was brought up in the Christian faith and resolved at a very early age that he would devote his life to the service of God, a life that to some seemed a waste of his abilities yet to him was complete fulfilment. It is a matter of good fortune for us that soon after his death his biography was written by a later Abbot of Iona, named Adamnam.

As soon as he was considered old enough, he attended St

Finnian's famous school at Morville where he became a deacon of the church. Columba visited many other monastic schools, increasing his skill as a verse maker and chronicler, becoming a skilled copyist. By the time he was twenty-four he was ordained as a priest. For the next fifteen years he worked as a missionary, devoting himself to organising and founding churches and monasteries throughout Ireland, recognised as a patron of Ireland alongside St Patrick and St Brigid.

Columba was a great collector of books and he borrowed a copy of St Jerome's Psalter from Finnian; Columba, without permission it is true, secretly made a copy of it for himself. Finnian, who had obtained the copy from Rome on one of his visits, claimed the manuscript copy made by Columba. The case to decide this ownership went before King Diarmaid, Overlord of Ireland. He gave a verdict against Columba and the copy had to be given up. The judge who made the decision said, 'To every cow, her calf. To every book its copy. Therefore the copy you made, Columba, must be restored to Finnian.' Columba resented this judgement and his resentment increased when his friend Curnan was killed after an incident at a hurling match. Columba was convinced that the followers of the king, who had made the decision over the Psalter copy, were responsible. These incidents caused Columba to make up his mind to leave Ireland.

He knew that the Christian Irish who had settled in Western Scotland were being attacked by the heathen Picts and Columba determined to help them, protect them, and then to spread the Christian message to the Picts themselves. In 565 Columba set out with twelve of his monastic brethren to find a centre for this work. In primitive boats they made the dangerous journey towards what we now call the Inner Hebrides and they landed on a small island no more than three miles long and one and a half miles wide. This was Iona. Near the shore they built their monastery, surrounded by an earth rampart as fortification. The chief building was the tiny church, built of wattle and daub with a thatched roof. The Abbot had a hut to himself while the monks had to share cramped quarters. As they acquired stock from the mainland they built stables, cowsheds, barns, stores, a mill, a kiln, a dairy and guest quarters. All the work stopped at regular intervals for the daily round of services finishing with a service at midnight. Part of their time was spent in copying and writing out the Scriptures and once the community was established, Columba, with perhaps a companion or two, set off for the mainland on missionary journeys in an effort to make the country more secure for the Christians. Their main target had to be the kings or chieftains of the tribes. If a leader could be converted, then their people presented themselves for baptism by the thousand. Columba succeeded in persuading King Brude of Inverness to become Christian, and from then on his work was less difficult. The heathen Picts came forward in great numbers to become follows of Jesus Christ. Columba and his monks ministered to all, influential and humble, acting as ministers, teachers, counsellors and friends.

Columba impressed those who came to him by his own life pattern, one of prayer, devotion and service. He was noted for the length of his fasts and venerated by his own monks. He seemed to possess the gift of second sight, anticipating events before they happened. He was wonderful with animals and birds with an ability to communicate with them in much the same way that St Francis did.

After one lengthy devotion, during which he meditated on Jesus Christ on the Cross, he looked up to see a robin resting in the hole in the wall that served as a window. He asked the robin to sing him a song. The robin immediately went into a lengthy song which Columba understood. The robin told him how he was in his nest near the wooden cross on Calvary on which Jesus hung. Jesus saw the robin and looked at him with such pain in his eyes that the robin flew across to Him, pressed his soft brown breast on Jesus's forehead and pulled out one of the thorns from the crown of thorns that had been pressed on Jesus' head. As the thorn was pulled out the blood of Jesus covered the little bird's breast. 'My breast is red,' sang the bird, 'because I was there when He died.'

When Columba grew too old and weary to walk about he was carried in a cart. Even so, he went on writing almost to his last day. The very last words he wrote were a translation of one of the psalms, 'They that seek the Lord shall want no manner of thing that is good.'

He went to the chapel after this and when one of the monks followed him he found that the chapel was filled with an unusual, soft light. Columba was prostrate on the ground in front of the altar. He was buried on the island but later, when the Danes threatened to despoil the monastery, his remains were taken to Ireland. The monastery on Iona was despoiled many times but each time Christian people rebuilt it. Iona is still the centre of pilgrimage for many Christians who go to pray to 'St Columba, tender in every adversity'.

St Margaret   (b. *c*.1050)   *10 June*
(In Scotland, *16 November*)

Most saints are people who have not married but Margaret, Queen of Scotland, is one of the exceptions. She was a particularly religious woman who exerted a good influence that was said to be felt even in her absence. It was also said that not only did no one say or do anything hurtful, unkind or irreligious in her presence but that no one near to her dared even to utter any word that was in the least impure.

Her father was Edward the Exile, next of kin to Edward the Confessor, who had been forced to take refuge in exile in Hungary when the Dane, Canute, conquered the realm of England. When Edward the Confessor regained the kingship of England, Edward and his family decided to return. Unfortunately, her father died and Margaret with her mother, her sister and her brother, named Edgar, stayed on to live in the court of Edward. The king was a religious man and the atmosphere suited the young Margaret who enjoyed the routine of prayer and worship administered by the Benedictine monks at the court.

The Norman Conquest disturbed this quiet existence and after a few years her brother, Edgar, moved the family northward where the King of Scotland, Malcolm, made them welcome. Malcolm had succeeded Macbeth, the Scottish king about whom Shakespeare wrote a tragic play.

They were given a home at Dunfermline where, although it was a royal palace, conditions were grim, bleak and uncomfortable. Margaret, by her example of goodness, kindness and spirituality charmed all around her and, in due course, Malcolm asked her to be his wife. Margaret and her sister, Christine, had intended to enter convents and lead a spiritual life, but after some delay Margaret became Queen of Scotland. Christina kept to her intention and later became Abbess of Romsey Abbey.

Margaret knew that her husband was rough, warlike and wild, but she saw the opportunity to show to their people a better, more religious way of life. This she did by her own example. She reformed the court and introduced a civility and respect for others that had not existed before. She brought books and learning into the court which had a wide influence on the Scottish people. Margaret's illuminated Book of Gospels now resides in the Bodleian Library at Oxford. According to an early writer, 'She incited the king to works of justice, mercy and charity. He, perceiving that Christ dwelt in the heart of his Queen, was always ready to follow her advice'.

Margaret won the respect and love of all who came into contact with her and she made a point of meeting the ordinary people. She would sit on a stone at Dunfermline and be ready to console, advise, or talk to any who wanted her help. Her gifts to the poor were extremely generous.

Every day crowds of poor people came into the royal hall and the king and queen fed each of them personally. Twenty-four people lived at her expense entirely and a little family of orphans was personally cared for by her.

On her journeys she always took money so that it could be distributed to the poor. Occasionally, if she ran out of money she would use the king's and he would pretend not to notice.

She was alarmed at the brutality of the wars which her husband fought, particularly against the English. When prisoners were brought back by Malcolm's soldiers, she did all she could to see that they were reasonably treated.

Although she did so much for others she had no care for

herself but fasted often and prayed long. A priest who knew her said that when she prayed only her body stayed on earth, her spirit flew to God. Even so, she was very practical and arranged all the ceremonial at court, and encouraged trade with foreign merchants. She reformed the religious observance of the Christian community and brought it into line with the organisation of the Church at large.

She had six sons and two daughters. Three of her sons were successive kings of Scotland and one of her daughters, 'good Queen Maud' married Stephen, King of England. Through her is descended the present royal family of England. She enlarged Dunfermline church and instituted there a community of Benedictine monks.

Malcolm, in his conflict with the English king, William Rufus, moved southward to the castle at Alnwick in Northumbria. There, Malcolm was surprised by William's forces and was killed in the battle. Margaret had fallen ill in the meantime and, on the day her husband died, said to her attendants, 'Perhaps this day a greater evil has befallen Scotland than any this long time.' When her son, Edgar, returned she asked how her husband and brother were. He, so as not to worry her, said they were well. She replied, 'I know how it is.'

After a final prayer she said, 'Let me be free,' and with that she died, four days after her husband. She was buried before the high altar of the Holy Trinity in Dunfermline church. She was named patroness of Scotland in 1673.

St Alban (d. *c.*209)   *22 June*

Alban is always remembered as the first person in England to forfeit his life because he was a Christian. For that reason he is referred to as the proto-martyr of England. We must admit that there are no contemporary records of his life and what we know about Alban was written about 200 years after he died, and then re-written by a historian called Gildas. This was again retold in Bede's Ecclesiastical History, in about 700.

Alban was a native of England, a prominent citizen of the important, busy Roman town of Verulam. We know a great deal about this town, for much of it has been uncovered and restored by archeologists and historians. It was large, busy, and a centre of civil and cultural life. It had a theatre, houses, shops and temples. The temples, naturally, were all devoted to the various Roman gods. The Roman officials had learned that there were groups of people worshipping a God who had lived on earth in the shape of a man called Jesus. They knew that this man had been crucified by the Roman governor, Pontius Pilate. Naturally, the Roman authority occupying Britain was suspicious of religions which threatened them and so did their best to squash any new movements. From time to time they would make things uncomfortable and dangerous for the Christians.

Alban took no interest in this new religion but was dismayed when some of his own countrymen were threatened for their belief. During one of the regular waves of persecution of the Christians, one of the priests sought refuge in Alban's house. Alban took him in and was impressed by the strength of his faith. Alban wanted to know more and in a few days he was prepared to accept this new religion. He was then baptised as a Christian by the priest.

The Roman authority heard about this and, fearing a spread of Christianity, soldiers were sent to arrest the priest who had sheltered in Alban's house. When the soldiers arrived, Alban had put on the priest's robes, covered with his large cloak, giving the priest other clothes so that he could make his escape. The soldiers were furious when they realised that they had arrested the wrong person, so they took Alban before the Roman magistrate. This Roman official was actually engaged in offering a sacrifice at the altar to his Roman god. He declared to Alban that, since he had helped a Christian to escape, Alban would be handed to the guards and receive the punishment in his stead. However, he told Alban that he would be freed if he bowed down with the magistrate and offered a sacrifice with him to the pagan god.

Alban refused and then proclaimed that he, too, was a Christian. To the Roman magistrate Alban declared, 'Your sacrifices are offered to demons and devils. Whoever offers such sacrifices will suffer eternally in Hell.' The magistrate was furious and ordered the soldiers to whip Alban with scourges. (These are whips with a number of lengths of leather, each having stones tied on to them. Jesus had suffered this punishment before His Crucifixion.) Alban did not flinch under this terrible ordeal.

The magistrate was so angry he ordered that Alban should be put to death for being a Christian, the first time such a sentence had been passed in England. His death was by beheading. The soldiers took him out and marched towards the river, intending to take him beyond the city to a hilltop nearby. The river was in flood and it seemed that the soldiers, Alban, and the vast crowds following, would not be able to get across as the water was too deep. It is said that Alban caused the river to divide so that all could cross. They reached the place of execution and, after a prayer, Alban laid his head down for the executioner to do his work.

As the Roman soldier who had carried out the execution saw the lifeless body of Alban, he cried out that Alban's example had so affected him that he, too, would accept the Christian faith, as did many in the crowd that day.

It must be admitted that one cannot be sure that this incident truly happened, for the earliest reference to St Alban was written in the fifth century by Constantius of Lyons who records a visit to the tomb of St Alban to whom he prayed for a safe return. There are no verifiable accounts of persecution of Christians in England during the rule of Diocletion, the Roman emperor of that time, but he certainly instigated persecution elsewhere and Alban could well have been a victim of a local uprising.

The Roman city of Verulam eventually crumbled when the Angles and Saxons settled in Britain. The spot where Alban died was still venerated in Saxon times and, indeed, King Offa of Mercia built a church and a monastery on this site. We know from the writing of Gildas that there was a church and tomb of St Alban in 429. When the Normans came they built a great cathedral and a new town arose, not called Verulam, but 'St Albans'.

St Etheldreda (d. *c.*679)

During the time that Britain was 'occupied' by the Angles and Saxons there were scores of relatively wealthy and high-born ladies, often related to the royal families of their day, who, answering the call they heard in the new religion, founded on the life and death of a Jew called Jesus of Nazareth, left their comfortable homes in exchange for the simplicity and poverty of the Christian convents and monasteries. In many ways this was a golden age of British national saints. One of the most notable of these devoted women was Etheldreda or, as she came to be known by a popular abbreviation, Audrey.

In seventh-century England, Christianity had already taken a firm hold in some of the royal households and one of these was the family of King Anna of East Anglia, at Ely. Anna, whose name nowadays we would assume belonged to a girl, brought his family up to be Christian and the example was followed by most of his subjects, if they knew what was good for them. In those days, if a king became Christian, inevitably his baptism was followed by the baptism of hundreds of his people.

One of his daughters was Etheldreda, a very beautiful girl, who took this new religion to her heart most earnestly. Etheldreda was born at Exning in Suffolk. She vowed that she would never be the wife of any man but would give her life to Jesus. Even so, she married twice in obedience to her father's wishes. First she married Tonbert, who died after three years. Then, her father, to remain on friendly terms with other powerful lords and kings surrounding him, made her go through a marriage ceremony with Egfrid, younger son of Oswy, King of Northumberland, but she made it plain that her duty as a Christian was far more important than her duty as his wife. The people around were amazed at her goodness and unselfishness and, knowing that she wanted to live as a nun in a convent, her husband allowed her to leave the court and enter a nunnery at Coldingham, near Berwick. After a period of study and service she came back to Ely where she founded a dual monastery which she governed for seven years.

Although so high born, she worked as the humblest of the

community. She confined herself to eating only one meal a day, wore only the meanest and most uncomfortable of clothes and denied herself even the smallest of concessions. On one occasion her neck came up in a great swelling which had to be lanced by a doctor. When the other nuns sympathised, she reminded them that as a princess she had worn jewels round her neck. Now, for the glory of God, she was pleased to carry these painful swellings.

She died in 679, buried in a wooden coffin in a common grave in the churchyard.

The story goes that at a later date it was agreed to take up the remains of Etheldreda and have them reburied inside the abbey church with a permanent memorial. A new stone coffin was found and the grave diggers took up the old wooden one. When the wooden coffin was opened it was found that Etheldreda's body was not corrupted, it looked just as it was when she had been buried years before. The only difference was that in place of the gaping wound in her neck, where the doctor had lanced the great swelling, there was now only the tiniest of scars. The Danes later destroyed the abbey church but this was rebuilt and became the magnificent cathedral at Ely. In the cathedral today you can see Etheldreda's story told in a series of sculptures.

As stated above, Etheldreda was popularly known as Audrey and, during the Middle Ages, many towns held a fair and market in her honour. The pedlars, of course, sold all kinds of trinkets at these fairs, many not worth the money given for them. This happens at markets and fairs even in modern times. However, when a youngster came home and showed off his purchase, parents would say, 'That's St Audrey!' and from this expression we get our word — tawdry.

In the church at Stanton Harcourt in Oxfordshire, a wooden screen was put between the nave and the chancel in about 1200. This was painted with many pictures of saints, but at the time of the Reformation they were all scraped off and dull paint daubed over the screen. Not long ago the paint was removed in order to show the fine woodwork. Evidently one of the panels had escaped the attention of the despoilers for, when the paint was cleared, a lovely painting of St Audrey was revealed!

To judge from the number of churches dedicated to her in England she must have been the most popular of all the Anglo-Saxon women saints.

St John the Baptist   (d. *c.*29)   *24 June*

In the calendar of saints John the Baptist must hold a special place for he was the man who first publicly recognised and announced that Jesus, Son of God, had come to men on earth. Jesus himself declared that of all men there was no greater prophet. John and Jesus were about the same age.

John's mother and father were Zachary, a priest of the Temple at Jerusalem, and Elizabeth, a relative of Mary, the mother-to-be of Jesus. Zachary and Elizabeth had been disappointed that they had no children and Elizabeth considered that she was now too old, but on one occasion when Zachary went up to the Temple at Jerusalem, he was chosen by lot to be the official who offered the incense at the great altar. As he did so he saw before him Gabriel, God's messenger, who intimated that Elizabeth was to have a child, a boy who should be named John. Zachary was amazed and asked that a sign should be given as a promise of this great event. Gabriel granted this request in a strange way, and to some extent rebuked him, for he answered that Zachary should remain dumb until the child was named.

Some months later the gospel story tells us that, in a similar way, Mary realised that she too was to have a child, who should be named Jesus. Mary hurried to tell Elizabeth about her child and it is evident that they were delighted about the coming birth of the two boy cousins, John and Jesus. Many artists have painted how they imagined the meeting took place.

In due course Elizabeth had her baby and, as is customary, many people suggested names for the boy, the favourite being that of his father. Elizabeth insisted on John and, when

Zachary was asked to write down his wish, he wrote 'John'. As soon as he had done this, his dumbness left him as the angel had foretold.

The two boys must have met often while they were children but later went their separate ways, Jesus to follow his father's trade of carpenter, John to live a wild life of a religious prophet, gathering crowds round him in desert places, always foretelling the coming of the Messiah and urging the people to give up wicked ways. He offered them a ceremonial baptism in the waters of the River Jordan as a sign that they were beginning a new, religious life. Inevitably, the people called him John the Baptist.

John's story is not only to be found in the Bible but also in the works of a contemporary historian called Josephus.

Jesus himself came eventually to John to be baptized in the waters of the river Jordan, not, as others did, to be forgiven for their wrongdoing, but as a sign that all of us need rebirth and the fresh start that forgiveness can afford. When Jesus was baptized, the onlookers realised that some remarkable event had happened for this was the beginning of the great ministry of Jesus.

John went on with his own work and, in particular, criticised the wrongdoing in high places, even at the court of the local ruler, Herod Antipas. Antipas was one of the sons of Herod the Great who had tried unsuccessfully to end the life of Jesus as a baby. Herod Antipas had married Herodias, the wife of his brother Philip, and this was against the marital laws. Because John the Baptist spoke out against Antipas, he was arrested and thrown into prison. Even from prison John continued to follow Jesus' ministry and to condemn the behaviour of Herod Antipas. Herodias had a daughter by her first marriage, a girl named Salome, who was very angry at John's constant criticism of her mother. On one occasion Herod, who was fond of the girl, rashly promised to give her anything she like to ask for. She asked for the head of the Baptist. He was dragged from his prison, beheaded, and the gruesome gift was presented to Salome.

John is remembered as the forerunner of Jesus and his feast day is observed on what is calculated to be his birthday, six months before the birthday of Jesus. The birthday of John the Baptist, celebrated on 24 June, is one of the earliest feasts to find a place in the Christian calendar.

Magdalen College, Oxford, incorporates what was formerly a church devoted to John the Baptist. Every year, on the Sunday after the feast day, a sermon is preached from an open-air pulpit in the college in John's honour.

St Peter (1st Century)   *29 June*

Peter, the foremost of the twelve apostles who followed Jesus, was not born with that name. He was Simon, son of Jonas, a Galilean fisherman. Simon followed his father in earning his living by fishing in the Sea of Galilee, as did his brother Andrew. He was a married man and in the gospel story there is a reference to the fact that Jesus cured his mother-in-law of an illness. There is a suggestion that his wife accompanied him on some of his missionary journeys, as there is also a legend that he had a daughter named Petronilla, but probably neither of these is true. His brother, Andrew, met Jesus before Simon did, and what Andrew told him about this new preacher aroused his interest. He, too, became enthralled by the words of Jesus and they both left their trade to become disciples. Jesus told them that with Him they could become fishers of men.

From the first, Jesus seems to have chosen this big fisherman to be the leader of his apostles and in so doing gave Simon his new name, the familiar one by which we generally know him. When Simon was asked by Jesus who he thought He was, Simon answered, 'You are Christ, the Son of the living God.' Then Jesus said, 'You are Peter (meaning stone or rock) and upon this rock I will build by Church.' So really in giving Peter a new name, Jesus made a pun, the name having a significance. At the same time Jesus declared that he gave to Peter 'the keys of the Kingdom of Heaven' and the power of 'binding and loosing' within the church. This seemed to give Peter a greater authority over the developing Christian Church than any of the other apostles had. When, later, Peter established himself in Rome he was regarded as the Father of the Church. He was the first pope, a word derived in a similar way to our word 'papa', meaning father. Peter was an impetuous, headstrong man, full of self-assurancce. He proclaimed his loyalty to Jesus with the words, 'Though I should die with you, yet I will never deny you.' In spite of this, sadly, he was doomed to deny Jesus three times, as Jesus forecast, 'Before the cock crow, you will deny me three times.'

When Jesus and the twelve went to Gethsemane on the fatal first Good Friday, after they had eaten together, Jesus asked them to watch for him while he prayed. Peter fell asleep with the others, only to be woken by the soldiers coming to arrest Jesus. Peter took a sword and cut an ear off one of the servants. Jesus prevented further fighting and healed the wound. The disciples fled, but Peter followed Jesus and the soldiers at a distance and tried to get information about the trial. Three times various people spoke to Peter and declared that he was a friend of Jesus. On each occasion, fearing for his own life, he denied it. As he asserted for the third time that he did not know Jesus, the morning light began to climb into the sky and the cock crew.

From a distance he must have followed Jesus who was carrying His own cross to the hill of Calvary, not daring to be seen. Only John stood at the foot of the cross as his Master died. Then, secretly, the disciples met in a room where they spent the rest of that Friday and all day Saturday.

On Sunday morning, when the women went to the tomb where Jesus had been buried, they found it empty and Mary Magdalen hurried to where the dejected apostles sat. She told them what they had discovered and John and Peter ran to the tomb. Of course John, being younger, got there first, but he did not dare to go in. Peter caught up with him and went into the tomb. Peter was the first to realise that Jesus still lived.

A few days later, Peter and some friends were fishing on the Sea of Tiberius. As they approached the shore, a man standing there called out to enquire whether they had caught any fish. When they told him they had not, the stranger said, 'Throw your nets out on the other side.' This they did and their catch filled the nets. When they brought some fish ashore they found that the stranger had built a fire and said to them, 'Come and have breakfast.' They recognised then that Jesus was alive again in some mysterious way that they could not understand.

This did not make things easier for the followers of Jesus. In fact, the authorities were more determined than ever to stamp out the Christians. For forty days the disciples hid in fear. Then they had a strange experience that changed their attitude. As they sat, not daring to show themselves, the room seemed to fill with a rushing wind. It filled them with a new, unshakeable courage. They knew that Jesus was in some way still with them and they went out fearlessly. They went out with new found spirit, the Holy Spirit of Pentecost, or Whitsun.

Peter was their leader and they made their number up to twelve again by voting Matthias into the place left by Judas. Peter stood up against the Jewish Council and was imprisoned and punished by them. He made miraculous escapes and travelled all over Palestine and Samaria, spreading the Good News of Jesus. Under the persecution of Christians by Emperor Nero, he was sentenced to death by crucifixion. Legend has it that he elected to be crucified upside down. His body was taken by his Christian disciples and there is a tradition that the bodies of Paul and Peter were at one time together in the catacombs under the streets of Rome, where Christians met for their secret worship. Some of the pious graffitti scratched on the rocks deep under the bustling city of Rome, still visible to visitors, would certainly suggest it. Personally, I was particularly moved to see these words, scratched nearly 2,000 years ago, 'Peter and Paul pray for Victor'.

There are abundant legends about Peter, one of which recounts that he was walking with Jesus one day when they came across a poor man calling on God to help him get his donkey cart out of a deep ditch where it had fallen. On his knees the man cried, 'God, please get my cart out of the ditch.' Jesus walked on and Peter wondered why He did not help the man. A little further on they came upon another man in an identical plight. He cursed and swore as he tugged as hard as he could at the donkey and the cart. Jesus went across and helped pull the cart free. 'This man deserves to be helped for he was trying to help himself.'

Peter is reported in one story as having met Jesus just before his own martyrdom. Fearing for his life, in a weak moment, Peter gave in to those who urged him to leave Rome. As he walked he met Jesus making His way into the city. 'Lord, where are you going?' Peter asked. Jesus replied, 'I am going to be crucified a second time.' Peter recognised that it was his own death that was in question, so he returned to meet his end.

For some time it was believed that Peter and Paul faced their deaths on the same day but there is no evidence to support this and the belief probably arose from the fact that they share the same festival day, 29 June.

St Paul (1st Century)   *29 June*

When Jesus died, hanging on a cross outside the walls of Jerusalem, the Jewish authorities felt that they had gone a long way towards stamping out the groups of 'Christians' who followed him. Surely, after such an example, these people would return to their former Jewish belief and observance. They were mistaken, for not only did the numbers of Christians in Palestine increase, but even in more distant places groups of Christians formed 'churches' or communities in which this new form of worship was practised. The Jewish authorities called such belief 'blasphemy' and declared that anyone found guilty of this charge should be killed. Among the Jewish officials was a man called Saul. Born at Tarsus, he inherited from his father Roman citizenship and his Jewish faith. He was brought up as a Pharisee and studied as a pupil of a celebrated tutor and Rabbi, Gamaliel. By trade Saul was a tent maker. In appearance he was not impressive, being short in build, with bandy legs, and he was rapidly going bald. Yet, in character he was gracious, and had been described as having the countenance of an angel. He was a fanatic about his religion and single-minded in his determination to have done with Christians.

When Saul was quite young he was present when Stephen, a deacon, was brought before the Jewish congregation, the Sanhedrin, and charged with 'blasphemy' because he was a follower of Jesus. Stephen was found guilty and Saul was among those who agreed that he should be taken outside the city and stoned to death, the first Christian martyr. Indeed, Saul followed the crowd to the scene of the execution and even looked after the clothes of the men who were to hurl stones at Stephen until he died.

After this, Saul set out to destroy the Christians, as he put it, 'to make havoc of the Church'. He discovered that this Christian religion was taking a hold in many parts of Palestine and, in particular, at a place called Damascus. Saul set out to visit that city and drive out the Christians. The journey must have taken several days and Saul had many hours in which to think as he trudged along the hot sandy track. He was probably puzzled at the fact that the more these Christians suffered, the greater was their faith. The more they were punished, the more resistance they set up. Not even the threat of imprisonment, or death, seemed to dissuade them. As the sun reached the highest point in the sky, Saul fell to the ground in what must have been a kind of fainting fit, yet he heard a voice speaking to him. It said, 'Saul, why do you persecute me?' 'Who are you, Lord?' said Saul. The voice replied, 'I am Jesus who you persecute. It is hard for you to kick against the goad.' Now, the goad was a stick held by the farm worker following a team of oxen as they ploughed or harrowed. If the creatures dragging the plough were slow, the farmer would urge them on with the point of the goad, digging into their sides. Saul knew at once what his conscience was saying. Already he must have had niggling doubts, pricking his conscience from time to time. He could not but admire the bravery and loyalty of the Christians and now, in one moment of time, he knew that he had been wrong. 'Lord, what would you have me to do?' Saul realised that the great light that now lit up his understanding had taken away the sight from his eyes. Blind, he could now see more clearly what was hidden before. He was led on to

Damascus and for three days he waited at the house of Judas, a shoemaker. Then Ananias, one of the leading Christians in the city, called on him. It was clear that he was not at all happy that one of the chief tormentors of the Christians was now to be favoured. However, Ananias, repeated the words he had been told to say and Saul regained his sight as swiftly as he had lost it. Now he became one of the most enthusiastic of the followers of Jesus and preached in the local temple. Moreover, he knew that his new faith could well end in having to give his own life for Jesus. He was a new man and, to show that clearly, he gave himself a new name, Paul. The first thing he did was to hurry back to Jerusalem to link up with the leader of the Christian community, Peter.

Naturally, the Christians were suspicious about Paul because of his former reputation but Peter accepted him and teamed him up with Barnabas and the pair of disciples visited the Christian communities in and around Antioch, travelling further north to Paul's birthplace, Tarsus, and even as far as Lystra. Lystra was a place where many of the Roman pagan gods were worshipped and many temples were built in their honour. Near the pagan temples a crippled beggar called Lucius sat and when Paul stood up on a block of stone, Lucius was almost at his feet. As Paul preached, Lucius grew more and more animated and then Paul called to him, 'Stand up on your own feet.' Lucius who was stirred with the excitement, leapt to his feet, a cripple no longer. You would have thought this would help Paul and Barnabas, but Lucius cried, 'Jupiter and Mercury have come to earth in human form.' Lucius gave credit not to Jesus Christ but to the pagan Roman gods. This was the sort of set back the early Christians had to face. Persecution, envy, failure, hatred and often death.

Paul carried out three principal missionary journeys all over the Middle East. Greece, Palestine, Syria, Asia Minor, Malta and Italy were within the compass of his travels. He suffered imprisonment, beatings, torture, shipwreck and house arrest. He experienced miraculous escapes but eventually, during a period of persecution under the Emperor Nero, he was arrested and condemned to death. As a Roman citizen he was not crucified but instead he was beheaded. Tradition says that he suffered death at a place called Tre Fontane, just outside Rome, and that his body was finally buried where the church of St Paul Outside the Walls now stands. There is also a belief that for a while both the body of Paul and that of Peter were hidden in the catacombs beneath Rome.

Before he died he wrote, 'I am even now ready to be sacrificed and the time of my death is at hand. I have fought a good fight, I have finished the course. I have kept the faith. As for the rest, there is laid up for me a crown of justice which the Lord, the just judge, will render to me in that day, and not only to me but to them also that love His coming.'

St Thomas More   (b. 1478)   *9 July*

William Roper, in his biography of his father-in-law, described him as 'a man of singular virtue', while more recently Robert Bolt, in the title of his successful play, used the expression 'a man for all seasons'. The two together say much about this brave and celebrated man who suffered death by beheading on Tower Hill rather than deny his own convictions and conscience.

Thomas was born of a well-to-do family, his father being a barrister and a judge. Before going up to Oxford University he was for thirteen years a member of the household of Morton, the Archbishop of Canterbury. After two years he returned to London, qualified as a barrister and entered Parliament. He was drawn towards a life in the church but thought himself not worthy of it. He married Jane Colt of Netherhall, Essex, in 1505 and they had four children, but the eldest, Margaret, was More's favourite child. the More household became the meeting place of the great scholars of that age and among frequent visitors were his close friends Bishop Fisher, Dean Colet and Erasmus.

A vital point in More's life occurred when in 1509 Henry VIII became King of England. His wife Catherine of Aragon had been married to Arthur, Henry's older brother, who had died some years before. The laws of the church forbade the marriage of a man to his sister-in-law, but special permission was given in this case. England at that time was, of course, a Catholic country, recognising the Pope as the head of the Church. Thomas More filled a series of high, important posts under Henry VIII, but increasingly found it difficult to agree with the king that he should separate from his wife Catherine and marry a young lady of the court named Anne Boleyn. The king was worried by the fact that he had no son to be his heir and, although Catherine had children, all had died except a girl, Mary. Cardinal Wolsey, after doing all he could to make the arrangements for the separation, failed to do so and was in danger of being executed, but died as he journeyed to meet the king. Thomas More became Lord Chancellor but failed to agree with the king about the legality of a marriage with Anne. The king was determined to marry Anne even if it meant separation of the Church in England from the Roman Catholic Church. Henry was resolved in that case to declare himself the supreme head of the Church of England.

Thomas knew that Henry would be extremely angry if he should oppose him but this did not make him turn from doing what he thought was right. He knew that he was in extreme danger and wrote to his son-in-law, 'Son Roper, I may tell I have no cause to be proud of the King's friendship, for if my head would win him a castle in France, it should not fail to go'.

The king had his way and Catherine was declared by an English court to be no longer Henry's wife. Henry immediately married Anne and she was crowned queen of England. More refused to attend the coronation. He was now out of favour with the king, so he resigned from the post of Lord Chancellor and retired from public life. However, he was now too well-known and too popular for Henry to let him retire quietly. Henry continued to hope that More would support his marriage to Anne.

Now the Pope was threatening action against Henry, and to counter this Henry put through an Act of Parliament which in effect created the Church of England with Henry, the sovereign, as head of the Church, denying the authority of the Pope. All servants of the crown now had to vow allegiance to Henry as head of the Church and this Thomas, together with many others, refused to do. Thomas was arrested and imprisoned in the Tower of London. For fifteen months he languished in a cell in the Tower, refusing at all times to acknowledge the king as head of the Church. His friend, Bishop John Fisher, was led out to his execution for so refusing and Thomas knew that his days were numbered. Nine days after Fisher's death, Sir Thomas More was tried in Westminster Hall for treasonably denying the king's supreme headship on earth of the Church in England.

He remained cheerful throughout the trial, often bewildering his accusers with his witty and penetrating answers. He even looked as if he might outwit his accusers except that he was declared to have had dealings with a certain nun of Kent who had presumed to warn the king about his wicked way of living. Finally, one who Thomas had considered a friend, Master Rich, later Lord Rich, told lies about conversations that they had had. At that point in the trial, knowing that his death was certain, Thomas said to Rich, 'In good faith, Master Rich, I am sorrier for your perjury than for my own peril.'

Even as he was led to the block, Thomas was cheerful. As he came to the foot of the steps leading up to the scaffold, he said to the officer, 'I pray you, Master Lieutenant, see me safe up, and for my coming down I can look after myself.' He arranged his beard carefully over the block, forgave the executioner for having to do his job, and said, 'Be not afraid to do thine office; my neck is very short, take heed therefore thou strike not awry.' As William Roper wrote, 'So passed Sir Thomas More out of this world to God.'

He was declared a saint and martyr in 1935.

St Veronica (1st Century) *12 July*

It seems strange that this woman, whose story is so well known and has such a wide appeal to Christians, may not indeed even have lived. There is no concrete evidence that there was such a person, or that the incident which has made her so popular ever happened. The story goes that as Jesus was led along the

Way of Sorrows, through the crowded streets of Jerusalem, to His execution by crucifixion on the hill of Calvary, a woman in the crowd was so distressed to see Him staggering along under the weight of the wooden beam, His face covered in dirt, sweat and blood, that she ran forward and taking a cloth, possibly the scarf round her shoulders, wiped the blood and sweat from His face. It is certain that, when crucifixion was carried out, groups of compassionate women attended and tried to comfort the prisoner, but there is no record that this particular incident happened.

The story gained belief, however, and additions were made to it. It was said that after this woman had wiped the face of Jesus she found an imprint of His face on the cloth and a veil said to be this piece of material has been preserved in St Peter's in Rome. So far as we can tell, this has been there since about 700. The name, Veronica, allotted to this woman is derived from the words *vera icon* — a true image, although this in English is 'vernicle' which is an image of the face of Christ often carried by pilgrims.

One story that gained popularity later was that Veronica had travelled to Rome to cure the Emperor Tiberias of some disease by wiping his face with this cloth. Many theories have been put forward as to who Veronica really was. One theory indicated that she was the wife of the Roman officer in charge of the execution of Jesus. This would seem to be an example of someone showing contempt for public opinion, as an officer's wife would be expected to support the action of the State, and not openly be seen to criticise it.

Another theory was that she was the wife of Zaccheus, the little man who climbed a tree to see Jesus pass because he could not see over the heads of other people. Jesus called to him by name and then went with Zaccheus to his home for a meal. Certainly, the wife of Zaccheus would have been impressed by this visitor and may well have been present as He went to His death. There is an account which suggests that Zaccheus later became a monk and that his wife, who might have been Veronica, helped to bring the message of Christianity to the people of France.

Another story tells that Veronica was the woman who was

cured of a serious illness merely by touching the clothes of Jesus. This is indeed the earliest version of the story of Veronica and is found in a document from the fifth century called, 'The Acts of Pilate' or 'The Gospel of Nicodemus'.

During the second century some Christians declared that they had identified the house of Veronica but it must be admitted that the evidence pointing to the existence of this woman is very slim.

When in later years the Christian Church devised the act of worship known as 'The Stations of the Cross' in which the people process round a church with the priest, pausing at representations of incidents which took place at the trial and execution of Jesus, one of the stations represents this incident, even though it is not certain that it happened.

Is it a deception then to celebrate each year on 12 July this incident which may never have happened and recall a woman who may not have existed? There is a case for this, since it reminds us all that we should, like Veronica, be compassionate towards all who suffer, particularly those who suffer from no fault of their own, but simply because they believe in what they are doing, even if the world condemns them and ridicules them.

St Swithin (b. *c.*862)   *15 July*

Most people remember St Swithin as being associated with a weather forecast. If it rains on 15 July, it is said it will continue to rain for another forty days. On the other hand, if it is fine on that day, then one can look forward to more than a month of good weather.

Swithin, however, knew nothing of this in his lifetime. He was born of noble, Saxon parents, and was educated at a monastery, passing his youth in study at The Old Monastery in Winchester. He became a priest serving the royal family of the West Saxons and was destined to serve three generations of kings. First he was chaplain to King Egbert who consolidated the English kingdom into one. Then he became chancellor and tutor to Ethelwulf who succededed his father Egbert. By him Swithin was appointed Bishop of Winchester.

The Danes were beginning to threaten the Saxons and it was Swithin who acted as tutor to the king's son, Alfred. There is little doubt that Swithin had a great influence on Alfred as he grew up and helped to mould the character of one of England's greatest kings. Swithin also persuaded Ethelwulf to free the churches and monasteries from heavy taxes and dues which were making the churches poor. In return, a charter was laid on the altar of Winchester Cathedral which appointed Wednesdays as the day on which services should be held, with the intention of praying for the king and the nobility.

Swithin was a practical man who not only built churches and chapels but also houses for ordinary folk and he made it his personal care to look after sick and needy people. On one occasion, a labourer happened to break a basket full of eggs belonging to a poor woman. The lady complained and Swithin restored to her even more eggs than had been broken.

Swithin himself led a very disciplined life, eating the plainest of food and as little as he needed. He travelled about on foot and asked for no fuss or ceremony when he visited the churches in his area. He was so humble that he asked that when he died, his body should be buried in the churchyard outside, where people could walk over his grave and where refreshing rain could fall upon it. Respecting his wish, this was done.

When William the Conqueror was King of England, Walkelin, Bishop of Winchester, caused the great new cathedral at Winchester to be built and ordered the removal of the remains of St Swithin from his humble grave into a place of honour inside the cathedral.

The day appointed for the removal of the saint's body was 15 July but it rained so hard on that day, and for the following forty days, that the coffin could not be touched. The people declared that this showed how much Swithin preferred to be out in his ordinray grave. The body of Swithin does now rest in the cathedral but the supersition survives that if it rains on 15 July, St Swithin's day, it will continue to rain for another forty days. On the other hand, if it is fine, then the fine weather will hold for forty days.

In some ways it is a pity that Swithin's connection with a weather forecast has overshadowed the proper veneration of the saint who played a historic part in the life of the nation.

St Mary Magdalen   (1st Century)   *22 July*

Mary of Magdala was a very beautiful woman often depicted with flame-coloured hair. Her story has been described as the most moving and encouraging inspiration in the Scriptures. We know very little about her early life but from the great deal written about her later life we can be sure that she was active, popular, lively and rather impatient about the customs of her time which seemed to limit women's place in life to the home, looking after house, family and husband. It is clear that Mary broke away from these restrictions and was seen by her neighbours to be fond of laughter, parties and the company of men. She liked having men friends, something which the other women envied and in their envy gossiped about Mary in order to give her a bad name, particularly with the Jewish priests. She gained her name from Magdala which was a small township on the shores of the Sea of Galilee.

We do know that she became great friends with the other women who helped Jesus and the disciples — Mary the Mother of Jesus, Martha and Mary the sisters of Lazarus, Salome the mother of James and John, Mary Cleophas and Joanna. Looking at the list one realises that Jesus did not only choose men to be his close followers.

The Bible stories certainly indicate that at one time Mary Magdalen suffered what we would call a nervous breakdown, 'a tormenting illness' it is called in the New Testament, 'being possessed by seven devils'. Jesus cured her of this by His calming presence and Mary became a close helper and friend from this time. She was devoted to His cause and felt that nothing could be too good for Jesus. On two occasions, as He lay on a couch at one of the meals He took with His disciples, she brought a pot of expensive ointment and poured it over

His feet, wiping them dry with her own long golden hair. The second time this happened Judas Iscariot, the treasurer of the group, was very cross about it and thought it a waste of money. 'Surely it would have been better to give the money to help the poor.' 'No,' said Jesus, 'you will always have the poor to look after, but soon I shall no longer be with you'.

Some authorities identify Mary of Magdala with Mary the sister of Lazarus who listened attentively at Jesus' feet while Martha, her sister, busied herself with the housework. Martha expected Jesus to support her when she criticised her sister, but Jesus pointed out that to be busy with mundane things was not enough. Mary, by her attention to His words, had chosen the better part.

When Jesus was arrested and taken before the various courts of Pontius Pilate and Herod, Mary must have been nearly heart-broken. But she followed loyally, not even denying her friendship with Jesus, as stout-hearted Peter did in a weak moment, or rather three weak moments.

When, finally, Jesus was taken out to be crucified on the hill at Calvary we know that four people stood at the foot of the Cross, unafraid to be seen as friends of the man just put to death. They were Mary the mother of Jesus, Mary Cleophas a relative, John the disciple who Jesus loved; and Mary of Magdala. Desolate, these friends of Jesus prevailed on a rich man named Joseph of Arimathea to provide a tomb for the body of Jesus, but since it was now the sabbath, what we would call Saturday, by Jewish law they could do no more than put the body in the tomb and leave any other normal procedures until the next day.

The reports do not entirely agree as to what happened the next morning, but sorting out the details seems to conclude that three women set out to clothe the body in ointment and linen cloth, but they found the tomb empty, no soldiers on guard, and the great stone which had been sealed over the entrance had been rolled away. The women fled in confusion and Mary of Magdala found the disciples and reported to them that the tomb was empty. Peter and John at once set off, running towards the tomb. John, being the younger, got there first but hesitated at the entrance until Peter caught up with him. Peter being the bolder, went into the tomb to confirm that the body was no longer there. Again, in confusion, they ran back leaving Mary of Magdala sitting in the garden quietly sobbing. As she sat she felt that a man was standing nearby. She thought it was the gardener and heard him say. 'Woman, why are you crying? Who are you looking for?' 'Oh, sir,' said Mary, 'if you have taken him away, tell me where you have put him.' The voice said, 'Mary,' and she knew that this was Jesus, alive again in some miraculous way, but certainly alive. She knelt and said, 'Master.' So she hurried away to tell all the other friends of Jesus about the wonderful happening on the first Easter morning.

For a while the disciples were afraid to go out and teach the Christian message but they gained courage and, within a very short space of time, the Christian church spread across the world as it was then known.

Mary accompanied John and founded a Christian church at Ephesus in modern Turkey and, while we have no confirmation of this, legend says that they married and that she died and was buried in that town.

St Lawrence (d.258)   *10 August*

St Lawrence is another saint, well-known from the manner of his death, but little-known for anything else. His popularity is proved by the fact that he gives his name to a river in Canada, a cathedral in Spain, a statue in Florence, six churches in Rome and over two hundred churches in England. His death, by burning on a gridiron, may have contributed to this popularity but his life must have impressed those who knew him, and other Christians through the centuries. This is surprising since we have few facts to go on.

He was born in Spain and from the first seemed destined for a career in the Church. He was good looking, courageous, intelligent and as a young man travelled to Rome where he served under pope Sixtus II who ordained him as deacon, just one rung lower than a priest. He quickly progressed to become the chief of the seven deacons of Rome and his work included caring for precious vessels and vestments as well as distributing the Church's alms and gifts to needy Christians in the town. But this was the time in Rome when unscrupulous emperors could persecute religious sects like the Christians and seize property, money and belongings of the unfortunates who resisted and proclaimed their faith.

Pope Sixtus was first arrested and tortured, but refused to give up any of the Church's possessions. For this he was condemned to death. The valuable property belonging to the Christian Church was now in the keeping of Lawrence who resolved to sell them or even give them away, rather than allow them to go to the emperor. When Sixtus was taken, Lawrence was heart-broken, and when they met for the last time as the bishop went to his death, Lawrence asked, 'How can you go to your death without your chief deacon?' Pope Sixtus, warned him that in three days' time, Lawrence would also be put to death, but in a much more violent way. 'Your battle will be fiercer,' the Pope predicted.

He was right, for as soon as it was known that Lawrence knew where all the treasures were kept he was arrested and imprisoned. We generally think of saintly people as being solemn and perhaps a bit dull. This was certainly not true of Lawrence. He had a wild sense of humour and it seemed that no ill fortune could dampen it. This sense of fun, combined with his earnest devotion to his Christian faith, impressed the jailer. Hippolytus, for that was his name, was so attracted to the faith that Lawrence professed that he and all his family asked to be Christian, and Lawrence baptized them all.

Lawrence was then brought before the prefect of Rome and ordered to produce the riches of the Church. His argument was that, according to Jesus' instruction, Lawrence should render to the emperor all temporal things and give to God all spiritual things. He declared that he knew that Lawrence had gold cups and candlesticks and all manner of treasure. Lawrence replied, 'If you will give me three days, I will bring you the treasure.' He was given three days of liberty to produce the riches. Lawrence first set about distributing the valuable items possessed by the church and when all the treasures were dispersed he sought out the poor, the crippled, the deformed, the beggars, the layabouts and all the people that were outcast from society.

They crowded into the imperial courtyard on the third day and Lawrence went to fetch the emperor. 'I have kept my word,' he said. 'All the treasures of the church are out in your yard.' The emperor was not at all amused. Lawrence was right in that to God, all humanity is treasure and Jesus would have cared first for the needy. This action meant death for Lawrence and the emperor devised the most horrible one imaginable. He was to be stretched out over an iron grid with a fire beneath so that he would burn to death as slowly as possible. Even the emperor's supporters turned away from the sight, as the heat beneath him increased. Even then Lawrence's sense of humour did not desert him. 'I'm roasted on this side,' he called to the executioner, 'to be well done, you should turn me over.'

As he neared death he began to pray for the emperor and the people of Rome. He prayed for the conversion of the city from its pagan ways to the truth of Christianity. Thus he died, and the Christian community buried his charred body in a secret grave in a field near the river Tiber. It is said that the jailer who became a Christian helped with the burial and was himself then killed by order of the emperor.

The bravery of Lawrence made such an impression that his death was followed by wholesale conversions to Christianity, and from that time there was a marked decline in wickedness in Rome.

The emperor who had ordered his death remained pagan but, within a hundred years of Lawrence's martyrdom, Constantine became the first Christian Roman emperor and he caused a church to be built over the grave of St Lawrence.

St Helen   (b. *c.*255)

There is a saying that 'truth is stranger than fiction', but when
we come to look at the stories of saints who lived long ago, we
often find that the stories that have grown up around the
popular saints are more entertaining and instructive than true.
We find that what was probably the original story has been
changed, or added to, not necessarily to deceive but because
oral tradition is open to error.

This is certainly true of Helena, or Helen as she is more
frequently called. The nearest to the truth about her is
contained in the writing of a contemporary historian,
Eresebius. He tells us that she was born in Asia Minor in
about A.D. 255. Her father kept an inn, which must have been a
superior establishment, for on one of his travels the Roman
emperor, Constantius Chlorus, met her, fell in love and took
her back to Rome to marry her. She enjoyed court life but
secretly disliked the pagan Roman beliefs and became
interested in the teachings of Jesus Christ. She had a son,
whom they named Constantine, destined to be the Roman
emperor when his father died. It seems that she was a very
virtuous woman and her attraction to the Christian faith
became more strong and eventually, when she was quite old,
she was converted and baptized into the Christian Church. She
influenced her son Constantine, so that he too later became a
Christian. In her old age she spent time and money in relief of
poor people and other good works. Constantius Chlorus had
by then divorced her to marry Theodora, step-daughter of
Emperor Maximium. The Emperor Constantine, who had a
deep regard for his mother changed the name of her birthplace
to Helenopolis.

She was nearly eighty when she set out for the Holy Land to
discover the true Cross on which Jesus died. The site of the
Crucifixion had been built over by Emperor Hadrian.
Constantine ordered the destruction of Hadrian's Temple of
Venus and the building of a Christian church worthy of the
most marvellous place in the world. Helen undertook the
search for the Cross. Three were found in a rock cistern near

the site, and one of them was declared the Cross of Christ. In 395 St Ambrose preached a sermon in which he declared — 'When Helen discovered the Cross she worshipped not the wood but the King, Him who hung on the wood.' Whether Helen did actually find the true Cross we cannot know but she certainly spent the rest of her days in Palestine.

That was the true Helen, but the less accurate story about her is worth retelling and has particular associations with Britain. Unfortunately, the story has no foundation in fact. Certainly Constantius Chlorus paid many visits to this country and, indeed, died at York.

On one of his visits to Britain he had occasion to enter the stronghold of King Cole of Colchester, in Essex. King Cole was noted for his extravagant way of life and the emperor enjoyed the time he spent with the 'merry old soul', his fiddlers and his jovial company.

Cole had a beautiful daughter named Helen who was secretly a Christian. Constantius Chlorus fell in love with her and, in due course, married her and took her with him to Rome. He knew of her Christian faith but while he could not believe in it, he was kindly and tolerant. He allowed her to bring up their son, Constantine, as a Christian.

Constantius died at York on one of his visits to Britain and his son Constantine became emperor. Constantine, although influenced by his mother, had not fully accepted the faith until on one of his marches to subdue a rebellion, afraid for the outcome of his action, suddenly, it is said, he saw a cross in the sky with the words *'Sub hoc signe, vinces'* (Under this emblem, you conquer). He then became convinced in his belief and confirmed Christianity as the state religion of the Roman Empire. So, in due course, the Christian religion spread to cover the then known world. All this was due, some might say, to a simple, devout daughter of that nursery rhyme character, King Cole. This story of St Helen is dramatically presented in a play-pageant by Charles Williams called *Judgement at Chelmsford*. Even so, Charles Williams expresses some doubt and writes, 'It was said once that she was an English woman and came from this country, now called Essex, or the land of the East Saxons, but I think learned men say that this is not so and that she came first from certain parts beyond the Danube.'

N.B. *Holy Cross Day is celebrated on 14 August.*

St Aidan   (d. *c.*651)   *31 August*

When Oswald defeated the Welsh king, Cadwallon, in a battle near Hexham in 633, he recovered the kingdom of Northumbria. He had been in exile on Iona where he had adopted the Christian religion in which the monks of Iona had instucted him. As soon as he regained the kingdom he sent to Iona for missionaries to help convert the people of Northumbria. They sent a rough, austere monk with a bad temper who did not last long. When he returned to Iona he reported that the people were rough and not inclined to listen to the Christian message. The monks of Iona met to discuss the situation and, at the meeting, Aidan blamed the monk for his attitude and mehtods. He said that people needed to be treated with kindness. 'When you first feed babies,' he said, 'you must first give milk and later on you give food which is more difficult to digest.'

The monks decided to send Aidan to repair the damage done by the other monk. Not much is known about him before he came to Iona to join the monks, except that he was Irish and had been a convert to Christianity. Aidan went to King Oswald who made him Bishop of Lindisfarne, on Holy Island, off the coast of Northumbria, north of Bambrugh. A man of great humility, Aidan, made this island, which can be reached at low tide by a causeway from the mainland, his centre of activity.

The king listened carefully and humbly to Aidan's advice and we are told that in the early days, while Aidan was not fluent in English, as he preached, the king would delight in interpreting and passing the message on to his noblemen. With the king's support, churches were built and the people flocked to hear Aidan and his pupils.

From Lindisfarne Aidan made all his journeys on foot, making his companions walk also. On these journeys they recited psalms, heard readings from the Bible and sang hymns to help them on their way. If Aidan and the monks received gifts they passed them on to the poor, the sick and the needy. If they were invited to a meal by a nobleman or local lord, they ate frugally and left as soon as the meal was finished to continue on their journey. A man of gentleness and moderation with a passionate love of goodness, he set a great example of Christian life. Whenever he spoke to the barbaric people of the region, they flocked to hear him and he gained many converts.

Aidan organised the monastery at Lindisfarne and accepted young boys who were given a fine education and were trained to be missionaries. The monastery had to be self-sufficient but no surplus was allowed to accumulate. Any money the monastery made went to feed the poor and to set slaves free. It was said by the people of Northumbria that it was not Augustine but Aidan who was the true apostle of England.

Oswald helped Aidan in many ways, both as patron and friend, and it was a sad blow to Aidan when Oswald died. However, King Oswin, his successor, was just as helpful and Aidan lived to see seventeen years of service to the people of Northumbria.

On one occasion King Oswin presented Aidan with a horse so that he could ride whenever his journeys took him, across rivers or rough countryside. Not long afterwards, a poor man asked Aidan for help and, although he was the bishop of Lindisfarne, he dismounted and ordered that the horse with all its trappings should be given to the beggar. When Oswin heard of this he was cross and asked Aidan if he could not have found a less valuable horse to give away. Aidan asked the king whether the child of a mare was more valuable than a child of God. The king accepted the explanation but with ill grace. However, after a few minutes he humbly knelt before Aidan and asked his forgiveness for being so unthoughtful. They then sat down together and the king was very happy. However, Aidan was sad and some of his friends asked him why. Aidan replied, 'I know that the king will not live very much longer.

He will be taken from us, for this nation is not worthy of such a king.'

When Oswin was cruelly murdered, Aidan was stricken by grief. He retired to a flimsy tent by the walls of Bambrugh Castle and there he died only twelve days later.

Bede wrote of him that 'He was a man of remarkable gentleness, goodness and moderation, zealous for God but not fully according to knowledge'. This comment refers to the fact that Aidan taught some aspects of the forms of service and observance of Easter that were Celtic and not recognised by Rome.

He was first buried in the cemetery at Lindisfarne but later his remains were transferred to the new church of St Peter. In Christian art the emblem of Aidan is a stag.

St Matthew   (1st Century)   *21 September*

Collectors of taxes were no more popular in the days when Jesus lived than they are today. Palestine, the land of the Jews, was occupied by Rome and Roman soldiers were on hand to enforce laws. There was no regular system of assessment, such as we have now, and often the collector was forced to haggle, bully and falsify. The tax collector did not go round from door to door, but those due to pay tax were compelled to go to the booth, or office, of the collector. With the information given the collector assessed the tax due. The collector had to make his living out of any surplus so that tradespeople and workers always suspected that the collector was cheating in order to get more for himself. Moreover, the tax collector was seen as a traitor to his people, working for the Roman domination of the Jews. The Jews even went so far as to consider that the homes of such people were defiled and would hesitate to take a meal with them.

Levi, the son of Alpheus, was the tax gatherer at Capernaum, an important town which was a busy centre for local trade. It was also on the road to Damascus, so that Levi was responsible for collecting road tolls. He probably made a good living at his work. Levi must have known about Jesus and he could have been in the crowds listening to him. The words of Jesus impressed him and it is quite likely that he admired his followers who had left home and occupation. He had also learned of the miracles attributed to Jesus.

One day Levi heard that Jesus was passing by his collecting booth and he made a point of being at hand when Jesus was near. As always, Jesus had a considerable following, who hung on every word he said. They must have been surprised and perhaps shocked when Jesus looked across at the despised tax collector and called, 'Come, follow me'. Levi left his job, his friends and relatives to follow the Lord. To give up his work was more difficult than it had been for Peter and the others. They could have gone back to their nets if it proved necessary but Levi could never go back.

It appears that Jesus called him by a new name, to suit his new life. He called him 'Matthew' which translated means gift of God. Bede describes the calling of Matthew in these words, 'He who called him outwardly by His word, at the same time moved him inwardly by the invisible instinct of His grace'.

The story of the call of Matthew is generally connected with that of a meal which Jesus ate at his home. Eating a meal with others was considered by the Jews to be an intimate, personal contact — in this case contact with a man regarded as a traitor. For this reason the Jews condemned Jesus' action. Jesus did not hesitate to challenge such an unyielding attitude and, when pressed to justify what he had done, said, 'I came not to call the righteous, but sinners'.

Jesus was probably in the second year of His ministry when Matthew joined the other disciples but, in conversation with Jesus and the others, Matthew gleaned enough to write his gospel. The accountant became an evangelist. His interest in numbers is evidenced in the repetition of seven and four in his accounts of the events in Our Lord's life. He retells seven parables of the Kingdom, gives seven words for the Pharisees, seven parts of the Lord's Prayer and seven blessings, or beatitudes.

Although the disciples were not concerned about money, they must have had to make some transactions in their day-today activities and, almost certainly, it would have been Matthew who kept the accounts. We know little that is certain about Matthew's life after the death of Jesus.

One contemporary historian emphasises that Matthew was more concerned with the conversion of Jews to Christianity, while other reports mention him travelling in Ethiopia and Persia. No great reliance can be put on these stories but he was probably put to death for his faith, far away from his original home.

St Wenceslas (b. *c.*907)   *28 September*

In the confused Europe of the tenth century, Christianity was by no means a protected religion for there were many pagan rulers who tried to eliminate it by persecutions and cruelty. Possibly that is why those who upheld the Christian faith, in spite of difficulty and danger, shine out as wonderful examples. Among these brave Christians were Borivay and Ludmilla, King and Queen of Bohemia. They had embraced the Christian faith but by no means all their family or the nobility followed that example. When Borivay died, his son, Ratislav, became king and married Drahomia, daughter of a pagan chieftain. So now the king and queen were pagan, but they did not object to Ludmilla bringing up their two sons, Boleslaus and Wenceslas, in the teachings of Christianity. Queen Ludmilla's chaplain, Paul, taught the two boys and eventually baptized them. Wenceslas was, therefore, well trained in Christian belief and practice. Unhappily, King Ratislav was killed while waging a battle against Magyar tribes that were threatening Bohemia, which left Drahomia to take over the government of the kingdom. With the support of the nobles she set up a pagan rule and threatened all Christians. In particular she was antagonistic to Ludmilla who was supporting Wenceslas in his efforts to extend Christianity. Queen Ludmilla was slain by some of the nobles supporting Drahomia, but there was such an outcry in the country against this cruel deed that Drahomia was driven out of the country and Wenceslas was proclaimed king. His brother, Boleslaus, fled the country.

Bohemia now had a Christian king and, as a result, the people lived in greater peace and security. The country became peaceful and prosperous under their 'Good King Wenceslas'. Wenceslas ruled with justice and mercy, punishing wrongdoers severely but having considerable regard for the poor and the sick. He forgave his mother and she and his brother were allowed to return to the court.

His devotions as a Christian once caused trouble with rulers of neighbouring countries. He was called with other rulers to a meeting with Henry I of Germany as president. Unfortunately, they were all kept waiting several hours before Wenceslas arrived. He explained that he had been saying his prayers. However, the other nobles must have forgiven him for he was so impressive in argument that at the end of the conference they wanted to give him a present. Wenceslas chose a very strange thing for himself. The meeting had been held at a place in Germany where the body of a saint called Vitus had been buried. Now Christians valued 'relics' of famous saints and so Wenceslas asked for the bones of St Vitus' arm. That sounds gruesome, but he took this relic and gave it a place of honour in a church dedicated to St Vitus in Prague.

But storm clouds were gathering, for his brother, Boleslaus, stirred up trouble among a group of nobles who objected to Wenceslas' Christian ideals. They invited Wenceslas to a so-called religious festival at Stara. Although Wenceslas was given a warning by his friends that there was a plot to kill him, nevertheless he was determined to go. Indeed at the feast he proposed a toast, 'To the honour of St Michael, whom we pray to guide us to peace and eternal joy'. His brother found no opportunity to attack him that day, but the next morning as Wenceslas crossed the courtyard alone, Boleslaus met him and said, 'I did my best to serve you fittingly yesterday, but today, this is my service'. With that he drew a dagger and struck Wenceslas to the ground. As he lay dying Wenceslas uttered the words, 'Brother, may God forgive you'. Friends of Boleslaus rushed forward to add their blows until Wenceslas was dead.

Wenceslas was proclaimed a saint and a martyr and his body was buried in a shrine in the church of St Vitus. The shrine of Wenceslas became a centre of pilgrimage and he was proclaimed patron saint of Bohemia which was later Czecho-slovakia.

It was much later, sometime in the nineteenth century, that a carol was written which is now sung regularly at Christmas time, 'Good King Wenceslas looked out'. It must be said, however, that the story of the king, his page and 'yonder peasant' has no foundation in fact.

St Teresa (b. 1873) *3rd October*

There must be many people who have the idea that saints are holy people who lived ages ago and whose deeds are largely legends rather than matters of fact.

Teresa lived less than a hundred years ago and her life story is well-known simply because she wrote a detailed account, not only of what she did, but also what she said and thought.

She was born in 1873 and we learn from her writing that she was born in Alencon, in the northern part of France, and that her father, Louis Martin, was a watchmaker. He was a very religious man and, when he was twenty years old, he wanted to be a monk. He was put off by the prior of the monastery that he wished to enter, and came to realise that his work was to be in the world, as a working man bringing up a family.

Unknown to him, at about the same time, a young girl, Azelia-Marie Guerin, was asking for admission to a Convent, so that she could spend her life as a nun. The Mother Superior of the Convent, considered her, but finally told her that her life was to be spent as a wife and mother, bringing up a Christian family.

The two met and married and had nine children, four of whom died quite young, not an uncommon thing in those days, while five, all girls, were destined to live their lives as nuns in convents, four of them, one of whom was Teresa, in the Carmelite Convent at Lisieux.

Teresa tells us that her parents set a wonderful example of Christian family life, setting aside a considerable part of their income for charitable causes and spending much of their time looking after people in less happier circumstances than their own. Teresa later wrote that her earliest memories were of smiles and tender caresses. Her father would help drunken men in the street, where others passed by in disgust. He saw a starving epileptic man at the railway station without the money to buy a ticket to get home, so Louis put what money he had into his own hat and then begged from passers-by for the poor invalid until he had enough money to set the sick man on to a train, with a ticket to take him home.

This whole-heartedness shown by her father was transferred to Teresa; it was the hallmark of her life. Writing about her spiritual life she expressed her attitude in the words, 'My God, I choose all! I don't want to be a saint by halves'. This was not to say that she saw herself as a saint, rather the reverse. She was speaking of her intention to be fully saint-like. Her later pain and suffering was accepted in the same attitude. She bore her suffering entirely without complaint.

Teresa (Thérèse, in the French form) was a frail child and when she was only four years old her mother died. Although she was brought up in the atmosphere of a very holy family, in her own story of her life she reveals that she was naughty and wilful like any other child, but was always very penitent after her naughtiness and sought to make amends. She admits to her great failure — self-love.

After her mother's death, the family moved to Lisieux to be nearer the home of an uncle and aunt who could help in the upbringing of the girls. There was a Carmelite convent at Lisieux and in due course four of the girls entered the convent. Her oldest sister, Pauline, became Mother Superior.

Teresa wrote in great detail about her own spiritual life and confessed to all the human failings that most of us experience, together with her sorrow at succumbing to them. She applied for admission to the convent at Lisieux but was at first refused as being too young. A little later she visited Rome for a papal jubilee. During the audience, when all the people knelt in silence for a blessing, she dared to break the silence and requested of the Pope, 'In honour of your Jubilee, allow me to enter Carmel when I am fifteen'. The Pope replied, 'You shall enter if it is God's will'. She was admitted when she reached that age.

Teresa entered the convent for a period of preparation before her final acceptance, or 'clothing' as it is called. This ceremony was fixed for January 10, 1889, and Teresa had hoped that it would snow on that day so that the ground should be clothed in spotless white, as she herself was. However, the morning turned out to be mild and sunny and the ceremony took place in the public chapel. She returned to the enclosure and as she turned into the quadrangle she saw that it was totally covered with snow.

She did nothing very spectacular and her life story as she wrote it is quite ordinary and uneventful. She wrote about her thoughts, her prayers and her life in a simple way, her 'little way' as she put it. She died of tuberculosis, after much suffering, at the age of twenty-four.

After her death, her diary, *The Story of a Soul*, was published and had spectacular effect not only among Roman Catholics but among other Christians and non-Christians all over the world. Many people attributed answers to prayers and miraculous happenings to her intervention and in 1925 she was declared a saint. At the great ceremony in St Peter's, Rome, when she was canonised, the great church was decorated with red roses. These were her favourite flowers and she had promised to send 'roses', a name she gave to miracles. As the Pope uttered the final words that declared her a saint, a handful of red roses, above the papal chair, detached themselves and floated gently to the ground.

Teresa has sometimes been called 'The Little Flower' and one of her favourite sentences from the Bible was, 'Whosoever is little, let him come to Me.'

St Francis   (b. *c.*1181)   *4 October*

Christians and non-Christians alike are agreed about the
appeal this man has made to them all through the centuries,
although some aspects of his life have been misrepresented and
exaggerated. What is overlooked very often is that the fables,
legends and romantic stories were the exterior elements of a
life devoted to Jesus Christ.

He was born in Assisi in northern Italy, son of a prosperous
merchant, Peter Bernadone. The child was christened John
but, as his father had a good deal of trade with France, and was
in fact in France when the boy was born, they called him
Francisco, 'the Frenchman'.

As a boy and a young man, Francis enjoyed the good life,
with numerous friends, lavish spending and entertainment.
Italy was a troubled country in the twelfth and thirteenth
centuries with considerable strife between rival cities. When
Francis, who had trained as a soldier, was twenty, after a
struggle between Perugia and Assisi, he was taken prisoner.
On his release and return home he fell ill and it was from this
time, Francis tells us, that he began to grow in spiritual
strength. He had formerly been generous and caring for less
fortunate people but now his care took on a spiritual quality.
He saw his life as being used in the service of Jesus Christ. His
reform was not complete until, hankering for the soldier's life,
he set out with handsome clothes and expensive equipment to
join the forces of Walter de Brienn. On the way he met a poor,
ill-clad beggar and Francis was so moved that he felt compelled
to change clothes with him.

Still Francis was unsure. He returned to his former
extravagant life but now with less pleasure. His friends asked
him if he were in love. 'Yes', he said, 'and I will take a wife
more worthy and beautiful than you can imagine'. He devoted
more and more of his time and money to caring for the poor,
he spent more time at prayer in churches, and gradually came
to realise that his social position and his wealth were a
hindrance rather than a help in life.

Riding near his home he met a man suffering from leprosy, a
horrible disfiguring disease. The man begged for money.

Francis gave him all he had and then took the man in his arms and kissed him. One wonders which was easier for Francis, to give all he had, or to kiss the man.

One day as he knelt before the altar in the church of St Damiano, just outside the walls of Assisi, he looked up at the crucifix and it seemed to him that it spoke these words, 'Francis, go and repair my church which you see is falling into ruins.' Francis imagined that this meant finding some money to do essential repairs at St Damiano. At the time, his father was away, so Francis took many of the goods in his father's store, sold them all and took the money to the priest at the church. The priest would not take the money and, when Francis' father returned, he gave his son a good beating, even though he was twenty-five years old. Francis' father appealed to the Bishop of Assisi for the money to be returned to him. People flocked to the church to see what Francis would do. The Bishop ordered him to return the money to his father. Francis went out, returned with the money, flung it down before his father and then proceeded to take off all his clothes and threw them at his father, indicating that he now owed nothing to him and said, 'Until now I have called you my father. Now I have no-one but my Father in Heaven.' Francis' father went off in a rage while the Bishop put his cloak round Francis. A labourer's tunic, like a long coat, was found for Francis who chalked a white cross on it before he put it on. In a sense, this was the beginning of the robe worn by Franciscan brothers ever since.

For some time Francis worked at repairing the church at St Damiano, living on the scraps of food he could beg. When that work was done he moved down the hill on which Assisi is built and repaired, and lived in the little chapel of St Mary of the Portiuncula. Portiuncula means 'little piece' and the chapel was on a little piece of land given to the church. Today this chapel is a tiny cell in the midst of a great church called 'Saint Mary of the Angels'.

A growing band of men who admired Francis and wanted to live like him grew up at Assisi and beyond, and in 1210 the Pope recognised them as the Franciscan Order. Francis sent out his brothers to all parts of the world. He said, 'I send you as sheep in the midst of wolves. Possess no money, nor coats, nor shoes, nor staff.' Their only possession was one poor coat with girdle, the coat marked with a white cross.

Francis taught God's love through the creatures around him. All were brothers and sisters to him. God's creatures seemed to recognise this and flocked around him and he called them by name, Brother Ass, Brother Wolf, and so on. He wrote about his friends in the animal world and has left us books of wonderful prayers that he used. The basic elements of his rule were poverty and humility. Francis never became a priest himself and there were times when he despaired even for some of the members of his order when they departed from the strict rules he had laid down.

In 1212 a woman named Clare met Francis and, inspired by him, she set up a sister order to work with and for the Franciscans. Their centre was at St Damiano and, in one of the dormitories, fresh flowers every day stand on the place where she slept.

The influence of the Friars Minor, as they were called, spread to Spain, Germany, Hungary, France and England. In all these countries monasteries were founded. In 1223, at Grecchio, the people asked Francis about making a living memorial of the birth of Jesus at Christmastide. Francis set up a 'crib' scene with living people and animals. From then until now it is a feature in most Christian churches to set up a representation of the scene of the birth of Jesus at Christmas time.

The life Francis led put a great strain on his health and he became quite ill. He meditated so much about the wounds of Jesus on the cross that the marks appeared on his body. Wounds appeared in the palms of his hands, through his feet and in his side, where the soldier's spear wounded Jesus. This strange phenomenon is called the 'stigmata' and there have been other great Christians who have had this experience. Francis considered it a joy to share the pain which Jesus suffered on the Cross. However, he did not wish this phenomenon to be generally known and from then on always wore gloves on his hands and socks and shoes on his feet.

Francis knew that he was very ill and he declared that he

would welcome, 'Sister Death'. He died in his little cell, the Portiuncula, on the plain below Assisi on October 3, 1226. Francis was one of those rare people who enter into glory in their own lifetime. It would be no exaggeration to say that he is one of the few men who all people, Christian and non-Christian, do not hesitate to recognise as a saint.

St Luke   (1st Century)   *18 October*

To put together what we know about Luke is like doing a jigsaw puzzle and when it is finished there are still a number of pieces missing. Nevertheless, Luke emerges as a positive, practical, man with great compassion and a considerable ability to record the events of the early days of the Christian Church. Generally, but without complete unanimity, Luke is considered the writer of the third gospel and also of 'The Acts of the Apostles'. From Paul we learn that he was a convert but was not a Jew, for Paul refers to him as a Gentile. He was a doctor, described in Paul's words as 'Luke the beloved physician', and in his travels with Paul there is no doubt that he was concerned with Paul's very poor health and ministered to him. More than that, he recorded Paul's journeys and had the ability to chronicle the early years of Jesus. In all probability he accurately recorded eye witness accounts.

The doctor of biblical times, maybe because the knowledge of medicine and healing was limited, had to observe much more than the clinical symptoms of his patient. He was expected to study climatic changes, the nature of soils, the habits and customs of people The physicians were the best informed people, and better trained than others in interpreting information. The doctor was trained to love and care for all kinds of men and women, he saw no bounds of creed or nationality. It is not surprising that with such training Luke found Christianity a religion easy to embrace.

Luke was a Greek, living in Antioch, and through him we learn much of what we know of Jesus' birth and early years. One feels that he must have been a close friend of Mary, the

Mother of Jesus, to have been able to include such a detailed account. Luke includes in his gospel Mary's experiences before and after Jesus was born. He tells us about Mary's journey to see Elizabeth and their joy at discovering that she, too, was to have a child, who was to be called John, a cousin of Jesus.

Luke describes the journeys to Jerusalem and also recounts six miracles and eight parables not mentioned elsewhere. In addition to his gospel, he told the story of the growth of the church in *The Acts of the Apostles*. After recounting the experience of the Ascension, Luke describes in detail the journeys and experiences of Paul. He was certainly with Paul during these journeys and witnessed Paul's work and miracles.

When Paul was nearing his martyrdom during one of the periods of Roman suppression and persecution of the Christians, Paul wrote to Timothy, 'The time of my dissolution is at hand. I have fought a good fight. I have finished my course. I have kept the faith. Only Luke is with me.' After Paul's execution, Luke went back to Greece to continue his work of spreading Christianity there. He died when he was eighty-four years old. The Emperor Constantius II ordered his relics to be transferred to Constantinople.

Luke had an important influence on the work of artists painting scenes of events that he described, because his work is so vivid. There is even a tradition, probably false, that Luke himself painted a picture of Mary, the Mother of Jesus. A writer in the sixth century stated that the empress Eudokia had in her possession, an icon, a painting of Mary, which had been painted by Luke.

Luke is symbolically represented by a winged ox. This probably is inspired by the sacrificial element in the verses at the beginning of his gospel. He is the patron saint of doctors and painters.

St Hilda   (b. 614)   *17 November*

The years of the sixth and seventh centuries in England were wild and tempestuous. In general the people of those days, from the families of the many regional kings down to the meanest serfs, were pagan in their beliefs and barbaric in their nature. Through the darkness, the lives of those converted to Christianity shone brilliantly, in particular the lives and example of the wives of the kings. These royal ladies did much to dispel the barbarism and, by example, show a new way of life according to Christian principles. We learn a great deal about these early saints from the writings of Bede, and one of them who died when she was very young was Hilda, whose early life was tumultuous indeed.

Her father was murdered by a rival, her mother fled from the country in fear, and Hilda was brought up by her uncle, Edwin, King of Northumbria. The fortunate thing for Hilda was that Edwin's queen was a Christian, and she brought Hilda up in the faith. Hilda was trained by Bishop Paulinus and was baptized at York by him when she was thirteen years old. At her baptism Hilda was told of a dream that her mother had experienced. Hilda's mother had dreamed that she was searching for her husband but found a wonderful jewel. This jewel spread a great white light over the length and breadth of Britain. This was the light of Christ. Hilda determined to do whatever she could to change the pagan land into a Christian land. She succeeded for six years while the Christian way of life spread and brought peace to Edwin's kingdom. But then came a reverse. Rival heathen peoples attacked Edwin's part of Britain. Edwin was slain, his sons were killed, his queen, who had influenced Hilda so much, was forced to find refuge in the south.

Hilda had intended to get to East Anglia where she had friends but Bishop Aidan called her to return to the north. He presented her with some land and persuaded her to set up a centre of monastic life. Hilda was then thirty-three years old. This work was so successful that, after only one year, Aidan asked her to take charge of a monastery at Hartlepool. Hilda had to take over from someone who had not been very successful but in no time at all she achieved such a reputation that all sorts of people with a problem said, 'Let's go and ask Abbess Hilda.' She advised on personal, domestic, practical and religious topics. She even helped somebody who had a plague of snakes and advised what to do when a community was invaded by flocks of geese.

Then she started what was to be her work for the rest of her life. She founded a double monastery at Whitby. This was to be a centre of monastic life for monks and nuns in adjoining quarters, each community supporting the other. This was a daring and original scheme but with Hilda in charge it worked. The name Whitby means 'The bay of the lighthouse', perhaps appropriate in view of her mother's dream.

Hilda was exceptionally successful in her management of the monastery. Five of her trainees went on to become bishops, the King of Mercia gave his one year old daughter to be brought up and educated by her nuns, and to crown all, the Church authorities chose Whitby as the meeting place for one of the most important conferences in the history of the church in this country. This meeting was called the Synod of Whitby.

It is not surprising that the Christian church which had spread throughout the world as it was then known, should not always find itself in total agreement. English communities were confused sometimes by conflicting orders that came from the two most influential centres, Rome and Ireland. They differed in many ways but one of the obvious differences was that the festival of Easter was held at different times. Hilda favoured the native Celtic or Irish custom, but when she realised that there were stronger reasons for agreement with Rome, she put aside her own preference and voted with her companions.

One very important member of the men's community at Whitby was a herdsman named Caedmon whom Hilda recognised as a great poet and writer of songs. Instead of saying, 'You should look after the cattle', she encouraged him to write the songs and poetry which have delighted English people through the ages.

For her last six years she was very ill, but refused to stop working. She died on November 17 in the year 680. She died at the daughter house of Hackness. Thirteen miles away a nun called Begu heard the passing bell in her sleep. She called the sisters together and they assembled in chapel to pray. They prayed till dawn when messengers came with news of the saint's death. After her death the Danes destroyed Whitby and the relics of St Hilda were either lost or translated to a place unknown.

Her epitaph should surely be something that was said about her by one of her nuns, 'All who knew her called her Mother.'

St Hugh of Lincoln   (b. 1135)   *17 November*

After the martyrdom of Thomas Becket, the king of England, Henry II, trying to show his regret for the part he played in the death of the archbishop, founded a Carthusian monastery, a 'Charterhouse', at Witham in Somerset, between Frome and Bruton. Henry had heard of a French monk, Hugh of Avalon, who had already been a Carthusian for seventeen years, and, impressed by what he was told, he sent for Hugh to take charge of the new monastery at Witham.

Hugh was of a noble family, his father was William, Lord of Avalon, a good soldier and an even better Christian. At the age of fifteen, he made a vow to become a monk. He ministered as a deacon at a small dependency of a monastery, often visiting the 'Grande Chartreuse', the mother house of the Carthusians which he loved for the quiet retirement of the place. Finally he achieved his ambition and became a monk. He lived a solitary life with a small cell and a little garden where he attracted squirrels and birds and a wild swan who fought off intruders.

When Henry II called for Hugh, he answered his call, and undertook the work even though he knew he would have to deal with a king who could be overbearing, demanding and bad-tempered. To counter this, he used good temper and firmness in his dealing with Henry. For instance, he learned that in order to make room for the monastery, Henry had turned out many villagers from their houses which the king then demolished. Hugh agreed to become Prior of Witham only on condition that Henry paid full compensation 'to the last penny', and built new houses for all those who had lost their homes to make way for the monastery buildings. Hugh held this post for seven years, often being called by the king to court to discuss matters.

As always, Hugh was glad to get back to his monastery with his pets and his swan. (Indeed, after his death when he was declared a saint, a swan was chosen to be his emblem.) However, after seven years as prior of a monastery, Hugh was called to be Bishop of Lincoln, the largest diocese in England. For a number of reasons there had been no bishop in Lincoln for sixteen years, so Hugh appreciated that he faced a difficult task.

In 1186, a great council was held at Eynsham Abbey, not far from Oxford, and the chapter were ordered to make a choice. Their choice fell on Hugh, and he was duly consecrated. Hugh undertook the work with energy, enthusiasm and a great sense of humour. The only thing that made him angry was injustice, even if it meant facing up to the king or the nobility. The ordinary country workers were often punished by the king's foresters whose job it was to enforce savage and unfair forest laws which protected the royal hunting grounds. He stood up to the king to protect the life and rights of ordinary people. On the other hand, he sometimes had to stand up against them, as when mobs raised a riot against the Jewish traders in Lincoln. He would face armed and angry mobs singlehanded to protect those who were being threatened. He even opposed the king's foresters if they laid hands on the land, homes or property of the poor. After one such incident the king sent for Hugh to give an account of himself. The king was then at Woodstock and, to humiliate Hugh, the whole court was told to ignore him. As Hugh came in, all the court suddenly turned their backs on him and carried on with their conversations. The king pretended not to see him and continued to sew on a bandage round his finger that had been cut. Hugh, remembering that Henry's great-grandfather, William, had been born out of wedlock to the daughter of a glove-maker in Falaise said, 'Now you look just like your kinsfolk in Falaise'. The joke broke the ice and the king became better humoured.

Yet Hugh became a very different person when he visited the sick, the poor, neglected children and old people, often travelling many miles in a day to be sure that all needful visits were made.

A monument to his work can be seen in the fabric of Lincoln Cathedral. It was Hugh who began its rebuilding and started the work which resulted in the beautiful cathedral as we see it today. He was a brave man, 'a good man, fearless as any lion in danger', who did not bluster. He dealt successfully with Henry II and later calmed the rage of Richard I when that king demanded exorbitant taxes. He refused Richard with a kiss of friendship and still did not pay the taxes. To refuse a royal tax was unheard of in those days but Hugh of Lincoln got away with it.

The effort he put into his work exacted its price and his health gave out. Worn out with fourteen hard years as bishop of Lincoln, Hugh died in the year 1200. He is one of the most interesting figures of medieval England and was described by John Ruskin as 'The most beautiful priestly figure known to me in history'. He was buried in Lincoln in the presence of two kings, two archbishops, fourteen bishops, one hundred abbotts, the Prince of Wales and hundreds of Jews from the Lincoln ghetto, who remembered the protection he fought for, for them.

St Clement (1st Century) *23 November*

The story that is commonly told of this saint is half true and the other half legendary, with some parts of it almost certainly referring to somebody else. In spite of that, there has always been a great affection felt by Christians for him and his name is one of those that is mentioned daily in the liturgy or service of worship in the Catholic Church. His likeness adorns many church walls, in particular there is a fine sixteenth-century mural in the church of St James at South Leigh in Oxfordshire, and Clement has given his name to churches all over England. For centuries in some parts of England his day was celebrated with a holiday. He was a slave, or servant, of the household of Flaxius Clemens and when freed took his master's name. He was probably a Jew converted to Christianity, for his letters show considerable knowledge of the Old Testament.

He became the fourth bishop of Rome, or Pope. After Peter came Linus, then Cletus, then Clement. He must have talked with the apostles and so is a direct link with Jesus. In one of his letters Paul wrote to the people of Philippi, 'I urge you to help these women with Clement also'.

He is best known for a letter he sent, about the year A.D. 95, to the Christians at Corinth when there seemed to be real division between the leaders of the Church there and other Christians who were not prepared to accept all that they were teaching. Never before had a pope interfered in the organisation of a local church, and the letter gave friendly, paternal advice. The letter is the first example of a pope involving himself in the affairs of a local church community. It was a fine letter showing firmness and care. The letter achieved its objective and was read aloud to the assemblies in Corinth for many years.

The letter opened by reminding them to establish themselves in peace, to renew their faith and set out the traditions handed down by the apostles. He then reminded the Corinthians how praiseworthy they were when they were humble-minded, but lamented their lapses into pride, jealousy and strife. He wrote, 'The sceptre of the majesty of God, our Lord Jesus Christ, came not in the show of power but in humility'. Clement's letter was a model for all pastoral letters, a reflection of Christian life.

Now we come to the part of Clement's story that is not so authentic. He is remembered in the church as a martyr, one who gave his life for his faith, but there really is no proof that this was the manner of his death.

The legend tells us that he was a cousin of the emperor and he managed to convert so many influential and noble people in Rome that the emperor was afraid that it would undermine his own authority. Accordingly, Clement was banished to work in the quarries of Crimea, digging out and breaking up stones.

Once there, the story is that, when the slaves were thirsty, he produced a well of water from the ground. This was followed by the conversion and baptism of hundreds of Clement's fellow slaves. The slaves then built churches for themselves and this angered and frightened the governor. He ordered Clement to be lashed to a great anchor and thrown into the sea. The slaves were appalled at this and wondered how they could recover the body of their heroic leader.

They went down to the sea and prayed until the sea parted, leaving a roadway out to a little shrine where, in a coffin, the body of Clement lay, still attached to the anchor. They say that for many years afterwards, on the anniversary of his death, the shrine of Clement could still be reached as the waters parted to leave a clear roadway.

In spite of the fact that these stories, and others which were told about Clement, were not based on reality, St Clement is still venerated for his connection with the sea and his emblem is an anchor. Many churches standing on cliffs overlooking the sea, like the one at Leigh-on-Sea which borders the wide Thames estuary, are dedicated to this saint.

'The Guild, Fraternity and Brotherhood of the most Glorious and Undivided Trinity', better known as 'Trinity House', has Clement as its patron saint.

St Catherine of Alexandria (No date)   *25 November*

Catherine is celebrated as the subject of perhaps the first school play ever to be written and a saint of such popularity that at one time in England her day was proclaimed as a public holiday. She has about fifty churches that carry her name and there are also numerous taverns which carry her picture on their name boards. Every child is familiar with her because one of the fireworks let off every Guy Fawkes Day bears her name, the Catherine-wheel.

Reluctantly one has to admit that in all probability there never was such a person. Her story is probably a mixture of

several people's lives. But it does tell of devotion and
courage and has been told through the centuries inspiring
others when faced with adversity.

One of the most charming versions is told pictorially in
eleven paintings in the *Book of Hours* commissioned by the
Duke of Berry, brother of the King of France, early in the
fifteenth century.

In the first picture Catherine, daughter of King Costus, a
beautiful girl, the admiration of all eyes, living in the city of
Alexandria in Egypt, sits in her study, reading a devotional
book, regarded and protected by a statue of Moses who
brought the law from Mount Sinai. This reflects the fact that
the body of a girl, said later to be that of Margaret, was
discovered in Egypt and was conveyed to Sinai.

The second picture shows Catherine confronting the
Emperor Maxentius who has ordered Christians to worship
idols. She astounds him with her knowledge and power of
argument. The emperor brandishes a sword to frighten the
girl. Catherine remains calm, holding a holy book in her left
hand while her right hand prepares to make the sign of the
cross.

The third picture depicts the fifty learned doctors and
philosophers brought by the emperor to overcome Catherine's
arguments. Much to the emperor's disgust, Catherine
succeeds in converting them to Christianity, and in a corner of
the painting we see how he deals with them. They are all
thrown into the flames of a great fire. In this picture,
unusually, the emperor stands while Catherine sits enthroned.

The next scene shows Catherine being forced through a
door into a small cell. He had promised to make her second
only to the empress if she would only give up her Christian
faith. Her reply was, 'I have surrendered myself as a bride to
Christ.'

In *The Golden Legend* which also tells this story, Catherine
had been severely beaten before her imprisonment, but in the
series of paintings in *Les Belles Heures* this scourging is the
subject of a fifth picture. Catherine is bound to a column while
the empress and soldiers join Maxentius to witness the
punishment. The scene closely resembles Italian paintings of

the suffering of Jesus when he was beaten before His Crucifixion.

The sixth picture shows angels who come to minister to Catherine and heal the wounds made by the whips. The empress had bribed the guard so that she may witness what is happening. She is so moved by this vision that she declares herself to be ready to be baptized as a Christian.

The next painting shows the angry Maxentius ordering that his wife should be beheaded for embracing the Christian religion. He looks sternly on while the headsman raises the curved sword. The empress is blindfolded, her long golden hair streams to the floor and her crown has fallen to the ground.

The eighth illustration depicts how the furious emperor has a great wheel prepared. It is a double wheel in this version and each of the wheels has sharp iron blades that will cut Catherine as they turn. Catherine kneels in prayer asking God to help her. Angels descend to shatter the wheel with hammers. Catherine is unharmed but three men lie torn and bleeding on the ground.

Unknown to Maxentius, the captain of the royal guard, Porphyrius, had been very moved by the conversion and martyrdom of the emperor's wife and he, too, became a Christian. He had taken the empress' body and given it a Christian burial. Maxentius heard of this and was furious. He tortured Porphyrius until he admitted, not only that he had been responsible for the burial, but that he was now a Christian. The ninth painting reveals the distraught emperor witnessing the beheading of Porphyrius and his guards.

Maxentius does not know what to do. He feels that he must crush this new religion centred round Jesus Christ which he sees as a threat to the Roman beliefs which raise up the emperor to the level of godhead. Catherine must die, he resolves. He orders her to be beheaded, and the tenth painting has this scene as its subject. Catherine's last words were, 'O hope and salvation of believers, O honor and glory of maidens, Jesus, perfect King, have mercy on me'. With these words, she died.

There is one more picture. Angels come down to take up her

body and transport it to Mount Sinai, a journey of twenty days, and there they bury her. It is said that oil from her bones flowed plenteously from the spot. Today an Orthodox monastery stands there. Alban Butler in his *Lives of the Saints* explains the origin of the account of angels conveying the body of Catherine to Sinai by reference to the fact that the garment worn by a monk was referred to as 'angelic' habit or costume and that sometimes monks were referred to as angels on account of their vows and way of life. It is probable that the story about angels carrying the body of Catherine merely describes the movement of the body by the monks to Sinai. This might also help to understand many medieval accounts of the works done by 'angels'.

The story of Catherine may not be true but it is worth telling nevertheless, for in those early days of Christianity many died for their faith. Indeed, to this day, some give everything, even life itself, because they are Christian. Catherine is a symbol of them all.

St Andrew (1st Century) *30 November*

Andrew was one of the Twelve Apostles, the first to be called to this work by Jesus. He was born in Bethsaida in Galilee near the shores of Lake Genesareth. The family must also have had a house at Capernaum for the gospels tell us that at a later date, Jesus lodged there. Andrew's brother was Peter; their father was Janas. They were a devout Jewish family but Andrew must have been critical of the formality of his religion for he quickly felt a sympathy for the wider teachings of John the Baptist. In particular, he wondered at the Baptist's words, 'Behold the Lamb of God', referring to Jesus.

After listening to Jesus, Andrew and another man followed him, beginning to recognise Jesus as the promised Messiah whom all the Jews were waiting for. Jesus sensed that he was being followed and turned to ask, 'Who are you looking for?' Andrew knew then that it was Jesus for whom he was looking and was the first to recognise Jesus as the Messiah, the Son of

God. He was the first believer, the *protoclete*, which is Greek for 'first called'. Andrew talked about this experience to his brother, Peter, and when Peter heard the words of Jesus he too became a believer. Both Andrew and Peter were baptized but they still carried on their work as fishermen until the day when Jesus watched them from the shore and, as they landed their catch, he called them to give up their work to follow him 'I will make you fishers of men,' said Jesus. They left their home and their nets and followed Jesus.

Jesus called twelve men to serve him, but Andrew is always among the first four when the apostles are mentioned. His name recurs in the Bible stories: when the great crowd of 5,000 people were fed, when Jesus preached to the Gentiles, and during the terrible period of Christ's trial and crucifixion.

After this we know very little about Andrew that we can be certain is the truth. Much of what has been written about him appeared hundreds of years after he died and accounts sometimes contradict each other. He is reported to have travelled to Scythia on the northern shores of the Black Sea. This would have been a particularly dangerous journey, for the peoples of Scythia were noted for their barbarism and ferocity. Andrew is said to have performed miracles which impressed them and gained converts. Another story tells that Andrew founded Christian churches in Byzantium, later renamed Constantinople. He even journeyed as far as Kiev in what is now Russia, and for that reason he was declared the patron saint of that country. The life of a Christian leader was always in danger, either from the wild peoples he sought to convert, or from Roman regime which saw a threat in this new faith.

The report of Andrew's death and the subsequent movements of what remained of him, the relics, cannot be traced back further than the Middle Ages but we learn from it that he was arrested and then tortured because he was a Christian and then was taken out to be crucified. He was not nailed to an upright cross, as Jesus had been, but bound to a diagonal cross and left to die, some reports say, upside down. He hung there, preaching and praying, for two days before he died. The relics were taken to Constantinople but, when the

Turks seized the city from the crusaders, the relics of Andrew were removed to somewhere in Italy.

A party of Christian missionaries determined to travel to Scotland in order to set up a centre of the Christian faith and, to protect them from the dangers that might beset them on the journey over sea and land, they carried a relic of Andrew. This may have been a bone or bones, or even some possession of the saint, a piece of clothing or an ornament worn by him. They survived the journey with no hindrance, quite a miraculous thing in those days, and landed on the east coast of Scotland. They built their church on the spot where they landed and the relic of Andrew was buried beneath the floor. That was the origin of the town called St Andrews.

The Scottish people adopted St Andrew as their patron saint and the national flag has a background of blue to represent the sea on which Andrew spent so much of his life, and the white diagonal cross reminds us that he gave his life for his faith, hanging on such a cross.

St Nicholas (4th Century)   *6 December*

It is difficult to account for the great popularity of this saint considering that we know so little that we can be sure is true. Legends abound and much of his popularity may well derive from the fact that his feast day comes conveniently in the season when the church prepares for Christmas and also that St Nicholas has been closely identified with Santa Claus or Father Christmas. His care for children and love of them has intensified this veneration.

He was born about 300 years after Jesus at Myra in a province of Asia Minor called Lycia. Myra was the capital city and the church was the centre of an area administered by a bishop. He was from a Christian family, inevitably being trained to be a priest. He was an outstanding priest and in due course became Bishop of Myra, noted for his extraordinary holiness and hard work. There seems to be some evidence that he was imprisoned during one of Emperor Diocletian's persecutions of the church. He also attended the great Council of Nicaea from which the Church achieved the Nicene Creed. He died at Myra and was buried in his own cathedral.

The first 'life' of Nicholas was written nearly 800 years later and its opening words are, 'Up to now the life of this distinguished shepherd of the church has been unknown'. The writer goes on to fill us in and it seems highly probable that what was then written is legendary.

The story goes that Nicholas was brought up in a strict Christian household and that his parents died when he was young, leaving him well provided for. He became Bishop of Myra and made up his mind to use his wealth in helping others. He heard of an unfortunate man at Patra who had no money at all and would have to sell his three young daughters to any one who wished to buy them. The poor man did not have the means to find good husbands for them. Secretly, at night, Nicholas took a bag of gold and threw it through the window of the man's house. The man was delighted, for he could now find a good husband for one daughter. Some time later Nicholas did the same for the second and then for the third daughter. The man was overjoyed but never knew who had provided the bags of gold. From this story it is easy to see the origins of the Santa Claus of today — the secrecy at night, the bags carried by Nicholas and the joy of finding unexpected gifts the next day. Link this with the fact that St Nicholas' day is just before the great festival of the birth of Jesus and we have the Father Christmas legend. Add to this the greater probability of wintry weather and the need to wear coats, possibly red, lined with thick white fur, together with the fashion for men to wear beards, and the picture is complete.

Strangely, the representation of the three bags of gold in the early illustrations made them look like gold balls, and this emblem was adopted by moneylenders, or pawnbrokers, in later years. Some other crude representations of the three heads of the daughters peering above the house gave rise to the odd story that the children had been pickled in a brine tub and were brought back to life by Nicholas.

According to legend, Nicholas must have been a man to contend with, for an account of what happened at the Council at Nicaea tells us that, disagreeing with another member of the Council, he walked over and slapped the other member's face.

Nicholas never gave way to paganism, even at great risk to himself. Three Christians had been condemned to death by the Governor Eustatius after he had accepted bribes to kill them. At the time appointed for execution, Nicholas boldly entered the prison and released them. Then he rounded on Eustathius with such vigorous argument that the Governor apologised.

Others in similar situations, persecuted for their faith, took heart from these incidents, in particular three Imperial Officers who had embraced Christianity. Nicholas prayed for them and we are told, the Emperor of that time, Constantine, had a dream in which Nicholas appeared and forcefully argued for the men's release. The men were released and Nicholas was asked to pray for the emperor.

From the twelfth century onward, devotion to St Nicholas grew. When Myra fell into the hands of the Saracens during the Crusades, the relics of Nicholas were moved to Bari in Italy where a new church was built. In the late middle ages over 400 churches were dedicated to St Nicholas in England alone. In Russia he is held in even greater veneration.

He is the patron saint of sailors who would look for the star of St Nicholas if they were lost, and often, instead of wishing each other luck, used to say, 'May St. Nicholas hold the tiller'. The story about the deliverance of the three officers was instrumental in making Nicholas the patron saint of prisoners.

It is very strange that a man of whom we know so little should command such wide-spread popularity. It was the Dutch Protestants of New America who were responsible for the translation of Saint Nicholas to Sint Klaes to Santa Claus and it was many years after that before the traditional Santa Claus or Father Christmas came to England.

St Stephen (b. *c*.35)   *26 December*

It is not a pleasant experience to feel that you hold an opinion
with which everyone around you disagrees. It is even worse
when the majority make fun of you for what you believe. How
much worse, then, if you are threatened with death and a
particularly nasty and cruel death at that. Death by having
bricks and stones hurled at you until you fall to the ground
with bleeding wounds and broken bones, then to suffer even
more pain from a hurricane of stones, until mercifully your life
ends. Most of us would change our minds and agree with the
crowd long before they got to the point of killing us. But this is
the kind of death that a man living soon after Jesus chose to
suffer rather than give up his belief.

After the death of Jesus on the Cross his disciples went about
the world as it was known then, teaching the Christian faith to
all who would listen and, indeed, persuading Pagans and Jews
and others to adopt the Christian way of life. Many Jews tried
to incorporate both the former Jewish and the new Christian
practice, meeting for their discussions in part of the Temple
called Solomon's Porch. Indeed such a group came to be
known as the Ecclesia or Church, a title that Christians still
retain.

It was inevitable that in a very short time the new followers
of Christ were seen to be rivals of the Jews and the Jewish
authorities could see that the growth of Christianity might
lessen their hold over the people. The Jewish teachers sought
to discredit the new 'church' of the Christians. The spread of
the gospel was left to the disciples who had followed Jesus and
some others appointed to help. To look after local affairs, like
the care of orphaned children, or widows left without means to
keep themselves, the apostles appointed officers called
'Deacons'. This was to leave the apostles free to travel and
pray and hold services. The Deacons were to be men of good
reputation and a man called Stephen was appointed to this
office.

Stephen was a tall energetic young man with a forceful way
of speaking and, in addition to carrying out his task of
distributing alms to the poor and needy, he took every

available opportunity to teach and preach not only to the Christian followers but also to the Jews, from whom he began to attract converts. Indeed, not only did he become famous for his words, but he gained the reputation of being able to work miracles, described by his witnesses as 'signs and wonders'.

Now the supreme rabbinical court of the Jews, called the Sanhedrin, accused him of breaking Jewish law and speaking blasphemy against the Temple. He was arrested and brought before the court. He was ordered to give up this new found faith called Christianity or suffer the consequences — death. Stephen showed no trace of fear but spoke up in his own defence. He traced the guidance of God in men's affairs from Abraham down to Solomon and ended by denouncing the Jews for deviating from the path of their own religion and allowing it to become corrupt and full of error. Moreover, he accused the Jews themselves of killing the Son of God when they crucified Jesus. Then the Sanhedrin brought in a series of witnesses who had been bribed to tell lies about Stephen. They reported that he had said all sorts of things that were contrary to Jewish Law.

Stephen rounded on his witnesses and on the members of the court with the words, 'Behold I see the heavens opened and the Son of Man standing on the right hand of God.' 'Blasphemy,' cried all the people. Hearing this word, Stephen knew that he was doomed. Blasphemy was the most terrible crime of which the Jewish court could accuse him. The certain punishment was death, outside the city walls.

Standing among the accusers was another young man, obviously respected by the court, for occasionally members could be seen talking to him and asking his opinion. This man was Saul of Tarsus who had been disturbed by the number of Jews becoming converted to Christianity. Saul had no objection to seeing Stephen suffer this terrible death. As soon as the court declared the sentence of death upon Stephen, the crowd dragged him through the streets to one of the city gates. Just outside was a rocky area which was obviously the customary place for such executions to take place. The walls and the ground were covered with the blood of former victims. Stephen was thrown against the wall and the people gathered rocks and stones of all sizes, ready to pound the life out of the prisoner's body. So that they might throw with greater energy and effect, the men took off their outer garments and, piling them together, asked Saul of Tarsus to look after them. Then they set about hurling rocks and stones at the condemned man. He fell to the ground with ghastly wounds caused by the stones, but still his tormentors threw at him. Even above the noise and shouts, Stephen's voice could be heard as he cried, 'Lord Jesus receive my spirit and do not hold my death against them.' Even in such pain and on the point of death, Stephen was able to forgive his executioners.

Stephen was not forgotten nor ever will be, for the church later declared him a saint and set apart one day in the year on which he should be remembered. One who gives his life for faith is called a martyr and the first to do so for any particular faith is a protomartyr. To commemorate this, St Stephen's Day is the very first day after Christmas Day.

St John (b. *c.*100)   *27 December*

In 'John, the Divine', we have one of the great figures of the early church. His title 'the Divine' simply means that he was a theologian, a student of man's relationship with God.

He and his brother James were fishermen on the Sea of Galilee, sons of Zebedee. Although John became a thinking man, when they were younger the two boys were excitable and quick-tempered, so much so that Jesus gave them a nickname, 'the sons of thunder'. As young men they were called by Jesus to leave their nets and follow him to be fishers of men. John was the youngest of the twelve apostles and Jesus seemed to have a particular affection for him for he is referred to as 'the disciple whom Jesus loved'. Mothers are always quick to help their sons and occasionally ask favours for them. The mother of these two young men once asked Jesus if he would allow her two sons to sit, one on each side of him. Certainly at the Last Supper it is very clear that John at least held the position next to Jesus. The gospels clearly demonstrate that he was rarely away from Jesus, but when he came to write his account of Jesus' life, it was very different from the other gospels. He tells nothing of the birth of Jesus but, after a profound statement about the nature of God, briefly describes the calling of the apostles and then recounts the miracle at the wedding where Jesus provided the guests with wine from water. Almost half John's story is taken up with the last week of Jesus' life.

He was close to Jesus at the Last Supper and it seems that, when their master was brought before Caiaphas, John and Peter were together in the outer courtyard, but John managed to gain access to the house itself, which indicates that he was considered a privileged person. Peter stayed unhappily outside, where he was challenged as a friend of Jesus and denied it three times.

John must have witnessed all the agonies of Jesus's trial; the flogging, the shame, and the cruel journey through the streets of Jerusalem out to Calvary where the crucifixion was to take place. Again it appears that he held some authority, for, while all the other apostles kept out of the way, John walked openly with Mary, the mother of Jesus, and stood by her while Jesus hung on the Cross. There were two other women there, Mary Magdalen and Mary Cleophas. It was then that Jesus asked John to look after his mother, treating her as if he were her son. From then until her death Mary lived at John's home.

After Jesus had died and been buried in the tomb provided by Joseph of Arimathea, John joined Peter, sadly wondering whatever they were to do. Saturday passed, and then early on Sunday morning they were roused by Mary Magdalen with the news that the tomb was empty. The body of Jesus had gone. Peter and John went racing off the see for themselves. John, being younger, got to the tomb first but waited outside. Peter came along later and, in his bluff way, went in. It was true. The stone had been rolled away and the body was gone. Later the truth about the Resurrection was revealed to them when Jesus appeared before them all.

Peter and John were closely associated with each other as they journeyed to spread the message of Christianity. John was with Peter when he healed the lame man at the Temple, and suffered imprisonment with Peter. They travelled throughout Samaria gaining converts.

The pillars of the early church were John, Peter, and James. The Christians were persecuted by pagan emperors of Rome — John saw the martyrdom of Peter and Paul, and many others. He was eventually captured but, possibly because of his age, he was not killed. Instead he was banished to the island of Patmos. Here he lived, preaching and writing. While we cannot be certain that he really was the writer, the books attributed to him are the Gospel of St John, three biblical letters and the book of Revelation.

When he was very old, John found it difficult to preach, yet crowds still assembled to hear him. He would simply say, 'Love one another, that is the Lord's command.' When asked why he always repeated these words he said, 'Because that is the word of the Lord and if you keep it you do enough.' The symbol for St John is a winged eagle.

St Thomas Becket (b. 1118) *29 December*

Thomas was born in Cheapside in London in the year 1118. His father was a merchant and Sheriff of the City of London. He was able to send Thomas to a school in Surrey which had been established by a religious order known as the Canons Regular. All went well until he was about twenty years old when both his parents died and he was left with little money. Thomas took a job in the business office of a relative and earned enough to live comfortably. One of his pleasures was to go out hunting and hawking, but on one of these hunts he pursued his quarry too energetically and fell into a swiftly running river. He was swept towards a great mill wheel, which was turning busily. Just as it seemed certain he would be killed, the mill wheel stopped and he was saved.

A few years later he gained a post in the household of Theobald, Archbishop of Canterbury and took the first step towards the priesthood by becoming a deacon. He so impressed Theobald that he was promoted to Archedeacon and was so highly regarded that he was consulted over difficult matters and was sent on missions to Rome. He came to the notice of the king, Henry II, and immediately a strong friendship began. Thomas was rapidly appointed Lord Chancellor, the highest position in the land next to the king. He was now extremely friendly with King Henry and their relationship was described as 'frolicsome'. Thomas was now rich enough to have a household of servants even greater than the king himself. On one mission to the French court, Thomas had a personal retinue of 200 servants, as well as singers, musicians, hounds, monkeys and eight waggon loads of presents. Thomas was a great fighting man too, proud, violent and quick tempered. Even so, he never forgot his religious duties, keeping a spiritual discipline of prayer and fasting.

When the old Archbishop of Canterbury died, Henry II wanted Thomas to take that office. Thomas warned the king that if he were to take such a position there might be occasions when he would have to oppose him. The king chose to ignore this and so Thomas was first made a priest and then installed as Archbishop of Canterbury.

Immediately there was a noticeable change in Thomas' attitude and his way of life. He gave up all the signs of wealth; he wore a hair shirt next to his skin and appeared in simple gown and surplice. He took on a rigorous programme of work with regular worship, prayer, meditation and reading. While providing good food for guests, he ate most frugally. He took a personal interest in all appointments in the church and in particular in the selection of candidates for the priesthood.

His first clash with the king occurred at Woodstock in Oxfordshire where there was a Royal Lodge. The king had instituted a regular payment there from priests, said to be for 'protection' but in fact it was an illegal tax. Thomas ordered the priests not to pay, which infuriated the king who declared, 'By God's eyes this shall be paid.' Thomas replied, 'By the reverence of those eyes it shall not be paid.' The payments were not paid! There were several skirmishes of this kind and every time the king was defeated.

Finally, Henry could bear this no longer and, gaining the support of some of the priests, called a council at Northampton. Here the arguments ranged against one another but, when the king finally challenged Thomas over his defiance, the priests behind the king called, 'Traitor'. Thomas knew then that his life was in danger and left the country to hide in France. However, the quarrel was patched up and Thomas returned to Canterbury in triumph.

Soon after this the king had business in Normandy and left the country. While he was away Thomas brought before himself some of the priests who had sided against him at Northampton. He proceeded to punish them with fines and imprisonment. Word of this reached Henry and he uttered the words familiar to all of us, 'Who will rid me of this pestilent priest?' It is almost certain that he did not want the death of Thomas, but four knights imagined that they would find favour with the king if they killed the archbishop.

It was just after Christmas, 29 December, when the knights reached Canterbury. They made for the cathedral and there was an angry encounter between the knights and Thomas with his clergy. The knights retired for a while as Thomas began a service but the monks, fearful for Thomas, closed the great doors. Thomas went and opened them saying, 'A church is not a castle'. Three priests stayed with Thomas as the knights came back. They shouted, 'Where is Thomas the traitor. Where is the Archbishop?' Thomas stood before the altar and said, 'Here I am, no traitor but Archbishop and a priest of God.' He was slain and cruelly hacked by the swords of the knights. The whole country was horrified and Thomas was immediately declared a saint and martyr. On his return, Henry II was forced to make an abject pilgrimage to Canterbury in order to calm the angry people of England.

A stained glass depicting the martydom was placed in a window at what is now the cathedral of the Oxford Diocese and chapel of Christ Church College. The head of Thomas, as it is hewn by the sword of a knight was positioned in one of the pieces of glass. It is interesting to note that a later king of England, Henry VIII, was also opposed to a Thomas who had been his friend, and this Thomas was executed by being beheaded. Henry VIII could not bear to see the representation honouring Becket, who had opposed his king, so he had the piece of glass picturing the head of St Thomas Becket removed, and a plain piece of pink glass inserted.

Further Reading

Attwater, Donald, *Penguin Dictionary of Saints*, Penguin
Books
Baring Gould and Fisher, *Lives of the British Saints*
Bede, The Venerable, *History of the English Church and
People*, Penguin Books
Duckett, A. S., *Anglo-Saxon Saints and Soldiers*, Macmillan
Ellwood Post, W., *Saints, Signs and Symbols* S.P.C.K.
Thurston and Attwater, (ed.), *Butler's Lives of the Saints*
Horton, Sybil, *Stars Appearing*, Hodder and Stoughton

Index of Saints and their Symbols

Index